M000210015

West Academic Publishing's Law School Advisory Board

———

JESSE H. CHOPER
Professor of Law and Dean Emeritus
University of California, Berkeley

JOSHUA DRESSLER
Distinguished University Professor Emeritus
Michael E. Moritz College of Law, The Ohio State University

YALE KAMISAR
Professor of Law Emeritus, University of San Diego
Professor of Law Emeritus, University of Michigan

MARY KAY KANE
Professor of Law, Chancellor and Dean Emeritus
University of California, Hastings College of the Law

LARRY D. KRAMER
President, William and Flora Hewlett Foundation

JONATHAN R. MACEY
Professor of Law, Yale Law School

ARTHUR R. MILLER
University Professor, New York University
Formerly Bruce Bromley Professor of Law, Harvard University

GRANT S. NELSON
Professor of Law Emeritus, Pepperdine University
Professor of Law Emeritus, University of California, Los Angeles

A. BENJAMIN SPENCER
Justice Thurgood Marshall Distinguished Professor of Law
University of Virginia School of Law

JAMES J. WHITE
Robert A. Sullivan Professor of Law Emeritus
University of Michigan

Advanced Legal Research

Ann Walsh Long
Head of Research & Digital Collections
Assistant Professor of Law
Lincoln Memorial University School of Law

A SHORT & HAPPY GUIDE® SERIES

The publisher is not engaged in rendering legal or other professional advice, and this publication is not a substitute for the advice of an attorney. If you require legal or other expert advice, you should seek the services of a competent attorney or other professional.

a short & happy guide® series is a trademark registered in the U.S. Patent and Trademark Office.

© 2020 LEG, Inc. d/b/a West Academic

    444 Cedar Street, Suite 700
    St. Paul, MN 55101
    1-877-888-1330

Printed in the United States of America

ISBN: 978-1-64020-748-6

For Jeremy and Abigail

Acknowledgments

Thanks to all the law librarians I have learned from and worked with over the years. Thanks also to all the law librarians who amaze and inspire me—many of whom I have tried to formally recognize for their efforts in this book.

Special thanks to Paul Hellickson, Alex Long, Sheryl Williams, Bianca White, Gordon Russell, Akram Faizer, Syd Beckman, Allison Starnes-Anglea, Andrew McRee, and my EPIC ski pass.

Introduction

Legal research can be costly for students and practitioners in two ways: time and money. The intent of this book is to zero in on the legal research resources necessary to meet the needs of the researcher at any particular stage of civil litigation. The goal is to help reduce the amount of time (and anxiety) expended during the legal research process, and identify resources that are worth every penny.

The *Short and Happy Guide to Advanced Legal Research* could be used as a text for an Advanced or Practical Legal Research course, as a supplement to a traditional legal writing or experiential course with a research component, or as a reference book to accompany a Continuing Legal Education seminar. It also offers an overview of the litigation analytics and artificial intelligence options available from Bloomberg Law, Lexis Advance®, and Westlaw Edge. In each chapter, research scenarios are provided to demonstrate how to find the resources necessary at each stage of the civil litigation process, *i.e.*, Phase I: Case Assessment and Development; Phase II: Discovery and Investigation; and Phase III: Pretrial Action. Examples of reliable resources will be included from the three major research databases (Bloomberg Law, Lexis Advance®, and Westlaw Edge), low cost resources (such as Fastcase), and authoritative free Internet resources. The emphasis will be on how to find what information is necessary in the most time and cost efficient manner.

My former life as a law firm librarian has prepared me to teach legal research in a manner few other law librarians and writing professors can. I have nearly thirty years of experience teaching and conducting legal research. During this time, I have worked at four large law firms and worked with hundreds of summer associates, new associates, and equity partners. Additionally, I have taught Continuing Legal Education seminars on free and low-cost legal research resources throughout the country for decades. My experience has taught me that legal research is not always a one-size fits all approach. Rather, your needs change depending on what you need and when you need it. Moreover, who your client is and what legal research resources you know about may limit your options.

Like so many things in life, legal research requires choices. When you have more time than money, you can look for *good* and *cheap* resources. When you have more money than time, you can look for *good* and *fast* resources. The resources I have discussed in this book are all *good*, but many are not *cheap*. In each chapter, I will provide a comparison chart of *good*, *cheap*, and *fast* resources. When a resource is *cheap*, it is free or low-cost. When a resource is *fast*, it is available online from your desktop or it provides a comparably huge savings in time.

Unfortunately, quality research services come with a price. However, price should not limit a practitioner's ability to conduct legal research and represent their clients. Legal analytics and artificial intelligence (AI) are now doing a lot of the work that was once only available to big law firms who employed lots of paralegals, legal assistants, and law librarians. AI can quickly compile useful information from large databases into visually appealing charts and graphs. Now that AI is doing all the time-consuming work of compiling the data, it is available to everyone, for a price. Most AI tools are still maturing and there will continue to be advances in this area.

I hope this book will provide a roadmap to guide you toward reliable research resources that are also *good*, *cheap*, and *fast* during each stage of civil litigation. As a time and cost efficient legal researcher, you will have more time to enjoy *not* practicing law. Although you can't buy happiness, you can buy a ski lift ticket!

Ann Walsh Long

Table of Contents

ACKNOWLEDGMENTS V

INTRODUCTION VII

Chapter 1. Top Five Questions to Ask BEFORE You Begin Legal Research 1
1. What Do You Know? 3
   a. What Is the Jurisdiction? 6
   b. What Stage of Litigation Are You in? 8
2. What Is Your Deadline? Alternatively, How Much Time Do You Have? 9
3. How Much Money Do You Have to Spend on Research? 10
   a. What Legal Research Resources Are Available? 21
4. What Are You Looking for—or What Is the Relevant Law? (*i.e.*, Statutes, Case Law, Regulations, Court Rules, etc.) 23
5. How Will You Know When to Stop Researching an Issue? How Will You Know When You Have Found What You Are Looking for? 26

Chapter 2. Litigation Phase I: Case Assessment Part 1: Is There a Valid Cause of Action? 29
1. Does Your Client Have a Valid Cause of Action? 31
   a. Secondary Sources—Treatises & Law Reviews 32
   b. Legal Encyclopedias, Jurisprudences, & Wikipedia 35
   c. Causes of Action, 2d 46
   d. Primary Sources—Statutes 51
2. Are You Prepared to Represent Your Client? 59
   a. Bloomberg Law Practical Guidance 59
   b. Lexis Advance® Suggested Questions & Lexis Practice Advisor® 61
   c. Westlaw Edge Suggestions and Practical Law 65

Chapter 3. Litigation Phase I: Case Assessment Part 2: Is the Issue Worth Pursuing? 71
1. How Much Time Will It Take? 71
   a. Time from Initial Filing to Final Disposition 72
   b. Fastcase's Docket Alarm and Analytics Workbench 77
   c. Lexis Advance® Litigation Profile Suite & Lex Machina® 78

     d.   Westlaw Edge Litigation Analytics 82
2.   What's It Worth? Jury Verdicts and Settlements 87
     a.   Lawyers Weekly Newsletters 87
     b.   VerdictSearch 88
     c.   Lexis Advance® Jury Verdicts and Settlements 89
     d.   Westlaw Edge Jury Verdicts and Settlements 91
     e.   Bloomberg Law Trackers 92
3.   Be Careful! Inaccuracies Abound! 94

**Chapter 4. Litigation Phase II: Discovery and
    Investigation.. 97**
1.   Depositions, Interrogatories, and Checklists.............. 97
2.   Finding People 103
     a.   Finding Public Records 104
     b.   Verifying Public Records 108
     c.   Monitoring People 113
3.   Finding Expert Witnesses 114
     a.   ALM Expert Directory 115
     b.   Lexis Advance® Context for Expert Witnesses 116
     c.   Westlaw Profiler & Thomson Reuters Expert
        Witness Service 120
4.   Judges.. 124
     a.   Almanac of the Federal Judiciary 124
     b.   Westlaw Edge's Litigation Analytics................. 125
     c.   Fastcase's Docket Alarm 127
     d.   LexisNexis® Context 128
     e.   Fastcase and Google 129
5.   Finding Public and Private Business and Corporate
    Information... 131
     a.   Bloomberg Law Company Litigation Analytics 137

**Chapter 5. Litigation Phase III: Pretrial Action Finding
    Pleadings, Motions, and Briefs.......................... 141**
1.   Federal and State Court Electronic Dockets 142
2.   Dockets and Litigation Analytics.......................... 147
     a.   Fastcase's Docket Alarm 150
     b.   Bloomberg Law's Litigation Analytics 152
3.   Artificial Intelligence 156
     a.   Casetext's CARA AI.................................... 156
     b.   The Future of AI: Judicata's Clerk................... 161

Chapter 6. The Ethics of Online Legal Research............ 165
1.   Competence... 165

2.   Cloud-Based Services and Third Party Vendors.......... 169
     a.   Data Breaches.. 170
     b.   Email 173
3.   Preventing the Inadvertent or Unauthorized
     Disclosure of Client Information 175
4.   Reasonable Fees... 177

Chapter 7. Research for Upper Level Writing.............. 185
1.   Finding a Topic 188
     a.   Circuit Splits 189
     b.   50-State Surveys and State Subject
          Compilations 190
     c.   Symposiums 196
     d.   Legal Trends 198
     e.   ProQuest Thesis and Dissertations.................. 203
2.   Get Pocket, Get Organized, and Create an Outline 204
3.   Preemption Search Strategies to Make Certain Your
     Claim Is Unique... 212
4.   Avoid Plagiarizing! 215

TABLE OF CASES 219

A Short & Happy Guide to Advanced Legal Research

Top Five Questions to Ask BEFORE You Begin Legal Research

Congratulations! If you are reading this book, you have made the decision to enroll in an Advanced Legal Research course. Every time I teach a Continuing Legal Education (CLE) seminar on legal research, attorneys tell me they wish they had an opportunity to take more research courses during law school. Pat yourself on the back for being ahead of the curve. Knowing how to conduct cost-effective legal research is a valuable skill that will benefit you in numerous ways. As a student, your legal research skills will help you quickly identify the resources you need to understand a legal concept, study for an exam, or write a persuasive brief. In practice, your superb legal research skills will save you time and money, because in the practice of law, time really is money. Attorneys make money by billing their clients for the time and expenses they invest in their client's case. If an attorney quotes a client a price of $300 to draft a will, the attorney assumes they will spend less than $300 in both time and expense (for this scenario, the attorney bills $100/hour, expects to spend one hour drafting the will, and $100 on the cost of research, making a profit of $100). If, however, the attorney spends more time or more money on legal research, they are no longer profitable.[1] Therefore, having superb legal research skills will help you be a more time-efficient and cost-effective lawyer. According to the American Bar Association (ABA), 49% of lawyers are solo practitioners, and an additional 20% work for a law firm with fewer than ten attorneys.[2] Even in big law firms, summer associates spend between 50-100% of their time conducting legal research.[3] As a lawyer, you will spend a considerable amount of your time conducting legal research, which is why you need to understand the process of legal research before you dive in.

When you begin your practice, your clients will hire you to provide them with the legal guidance and expertise they need. What should you do first? Ask A LOT of questions! Ask your client a lot of questions about their situation and ask yourself a lot of questions about your ability to satisfactorily represent your client. Every attorney was once in your newbie shoes and agreed to take on a case requiring research in an unfamiliar or new area of the law. Some of these attorneys later became experts in their field and have taken the time to write an article or compile a treatise in their area of expertise. The first step of the legal research process is to find out what information is already available to assist you with your understanding of client's legal issues.

For legal research, if knowing where to look is half the battle, knowing what you are looking for is the other half. Ask the following

---

[1]   In case you are wondering, it is unlikely that an attorney would later bill his client for more than the original quote. Would you pay someone more to paint your house if they originally miscalculated how many gallons of paint were needed?

[2]   *Lawyer Demographics*, ABA DEFENDING LIBERTY PURSUING JUSTICE (2013), https://www.americanbar.org/content/dam/aba/migrated/marketresearch/Public Documents/lawyer_demographics_2013.authcheckdam.pdf. The ABA no longer reports statistics on law firm size.

[3]   *Summer Associates Identify Writing and Legal Research Skills Required on the Job*, LEXISNEXIS INSIGHTS (2016), available at: http://www.lexisnexis.com/documents/pdf/20161109032544_large.pdf.

five questions BEFORE you begin research to ensure that you fully understand what you are looking for. Otherwise, you may waste a lot of time Googling around trying to figure out what could be easily identified if only you would have taken the time to anticipate what you may need. Knowing the answer to the following questions will start you off on the right path and ultimately, save you time and money.

Here are the top five questions you should ask before you begin legal research:

1. **What do you know?** What is the jurisdiction, and what stage of litigation are you in?

2. **What is the deadline?** Alternatively, how much time do you have?

3. **How much money is available to spend on legal research and what legal research resources are available?**

4. **What are you looking for—or what is the relevant law?** (*i.e.*, statutes, case law, regulations, court rules, etc.)

5. **When will you know when to stop researching an issue? How will you know when you have found what you are looking for?**

1. What Do You Know?

Let's start at the beginning. When you begin to research a client's issue, there is usually another attorney who knows more about the subject than you do. Your first job is to find out everything about the client's issue, and then ask additional follow up questions. You may be talking directly to your client, or a partner may have assigned the research to you. During the initial client interview, your client will tell you about their legal issue. This is an opportunity for you to find out if the client's issue is a legal matter worth pursuing. For example, your approach will be very different if your client is an insurance company vs. an individual suing their insurance company. The former may restrict your legal research options, while the latter may restrict the type of action you can pursue. You need to consider how much time and effort you expect to spend on the case and then determine whether the issue is worth pursuing.

This is where all of those doctrinal course outlines you have created will pay off. As your client tells you their story, you should be busy thinking about the rules you have learned in law school and the various exceptions to those rules. It is your job to ask as many questions as you can to decide if your client has a valid cause of action. This will be covered more in the next chapter, but learning about a client's legal issue is just the beginning.

Has the client filled out an intake form? Most law firms have a New Client Intake form, but, if you need an example, look for one on either Lexis Advance®[4] or Westlaw Edge.[5] Your local bar association may also offer guidance on how to evaluate new clients[6] and provide sample forms on their websites or in bar journals. The American Bar Association (ABA) provides a wealth of information, including a newsletter aimed at solo and small law firms called GPSolo.[7] Additionally, there is a Solo/Small Firms Forms Library available on the ABA's website.[8] If you are wondering what types of

---

[4]   The author has an academic account for Bloomberg Law, Fastcase, Lexis Advance®, and Westlaw Edge.

[5]   On the Lexis Advance® homepage, select the Content Type tab, then select Forms, then narrow by State or Practice Area. On Westlaw, select the All Content tab, then select Forms, then narrow by State, Topic, or Publication. On either service, conduct a general search of all forms for "new client intake" to view examples.

[6]   TENNESSEE BAR ASSOCIATION, *Case Acceptance and Client Screening*, https://www.tba.org/case-acceptance-and-client-screening.

[7]   Recent issues of the GPSolo Magazine is available online at: https://www.americanbar.org/groups/gpsolo/publications/gp_solo/. A subscription to *GPSolo* magazine is included with a $60 annual membership in the Solo, Small Firm, and General Practice Division.

[8]   Visit   https://www.americanbar.org/groups/gpsolo/resources/solo_small_firm_formslibrary.html to access the forms available in the Advising Small Business

information you need, these forms may provide you with a good starting point. At the very least, a new client intake form should include the client's full legal name, social security number, and current address. Proof of identification, such as a driver's license or passport, should always be required. There may also be space for your client to describe their issue.

Before you begin any research, find out how the firm (or determine how you) will recover your time and research expenses. There are several methods for charging for your legal services. Two of the most popular methods are through a flat-rate agreement or through a billable hour rate.[9] The setting of fees and the discussion of a payment schedule can be uncomfortable, but is a necessary conversation to have with your clients. Knowing that you have a full understanding of how much time you expect to spend on their legal issue is paramount to a client's satisfaction (and your ability to keep the lights on!). Even if you are taking on a client's case on a contingency fee basis or pro bono, keep track of the hours you spend. If you are successful in court, reasonable attorney's fees may be awarded at the judge's discretion, which makes it imperative to keep detailed records on your billable hours. Law firms typically assign numbers to clients and sub-numbers for each matter the firm will handle. For example, if you have a family law practice and a client has hired you to represent them in a divorce, the firm would assign a client and matter number—something like 319101-00001. If that same client also needs the firm to draft a new will, the client number would remain the same, but a new matter number would be created—319101-00002. Numbers are used to help keep client records confidential. Instead of labeling files as "Jones—Divorce" or

---

Library and the Estate Planning Library. There are several sample intake forms in the Estate Planning Library, including: family questionnaire, asset questionnaire, engagement letter for individual, engagement letter for couple, additional terms and conditions of client employment, and a privacy notice.

   [9]   This book will focus on how to conduct cost-effective research and as such, will discuss either billable time or flat-rate models to recover research expenses.

"Jones—Will", most firms use a numerical system to keep track of their client's files and prevent the consequences of unintentionally disclosing client confidences.[10]

Your firm may require entering a valid client matter number before logging on to any fee based research service. This requirement helps law firms recover online legal research expenses. If you have not decided whether your client has a valid cause of action, you may want to use free or low cost legal research services. Determining whether your client has a valid cause of action may require several hours of research; the process of which will be discussed in the next chapter. At the beginning of representation, you need to identify the client's legal issue, and then ask additional questions that will assist you with research.

a.   *What Is the Jurisdiction?*

Once you have a general understanding of your client's issue, you need to determine whether it will likely be resolved through litigation in a state or federal court system.[11] If it is a state issue, which state's law will apply? Never assume the jurisdiction based on where you meet your client! For example, if your client wants to hire you to represent them in a divorce, it is possible that they have recently moved to a new state before talking with you. Knowing when and where your client's legal issue occurred will be one piece of the jurisdictional puzzle. Review the information on the new client intake sheet to verify your client's domicile. Assuming all of the information is correct and you have determined that your client's issue can be resolved through the process of litigation in

---

[10]   MODEL RULES OF PROF'L CONDUCT r. 1.1 (AM. BAR ASS'N 2018). The ethics of legal research will be discussed in the Ethics of Legal Research chapter.

[11]   Some issues require review from an administrative agency prior to litigation. For example, if you want to file an employment discrimination lawsuit, your first step begins by filing an administrative charge with the Equal Employment Opportunity Commission (EEOC). If you skip this step and file directly with a court, you may have your lawsuit dismissed for failing to exhaust your administrative remedies.

either a state or federal court, then consider if you have any venue options. The second piece of the jurisdictional puzzle is to determine whether the obvious or closest court will provide the best outcome for your client.

Consider whether your client's action might receive more favorable treatment in a different venue. A few years ago, the University of Tennessee (UT) was sued in the Western District of Tennessee, which is located in Nashville. UT's main campus is located in Knoxville, just a few miles away from the Eastern District Court of Tennessee, which one would assume is the more likely venue. However, the plaintiff's attorneys chose the Nashville location because they were trying to get a jury that might be less prejudicial than most residents who live in Knoxville and cheer for the Vols[12] every weekend. Additionally, your client might have a more favorable outcome in a federal, rather than a state court.[13] Some state laws are near verbatim adoptions of federal law, but may differ on certain specifications.[14] If you believe you have options, research the various laws and how the judges in each of

---

[12]   Tennessee is known as the "Volunteer State." During the War of 1812, a large number of soldiers from Tennessee volunteered to fight. Later, the University of Tennessee adopted The Volunteers (or Vols) as the university's nickname.

[13]   For a thorough examination of civil procedure issues, I recommend two treatises that cover federal civil procedure in depth: MOORE'S FEDERAL PRACTICE and FEDERAL PRACTICE AND PROCEDURE (commonly referred to as "Wright & Miller"). MOORE'S FEDERAL PRACTICE offers a civil and criminal treatise and is available on Lexis Advance®. Volume 17A of the civil treatise has several chapters analyzing State and Federal Courts, chapters 120-124. FEDERAL PRACTICE AND PROCEDURE is available on Westlaw. Expand the contents and browse the chapters in the *Federal Practice Deskbook,* especially Chapter 8: The Relations Between State and Federal Courts.

[14]   Consider the similarities between state and federal employment discrimination laws. "Title VII of the Civil Rights Act of 1964 prohibits public and private employment discrimination based on sex, race, color, religion, or national origin in hiring or firing, compensation, terms, conditions, or privileges of employment." 42 U.S.C. § 2000e-7 (2018). This statute expressly permits states to enact non-conflicting fair employment practice laws, similar to Title VII, where state law supplements or coexists with federal employment discrimination laws. Id.

those jurisdictions have decided cases similar to your client's to determine the most favorable option for your client.[15]

b.   *What Stage of Litigation Are You in?*

Not all legal research projects start at the beginning. If you are working in a law firm, make sure you do not duplicate efforts previously billed to the client.[16] Ask the assigning partner what stage of litigation you are in or do a bit of research to find out. Most law firms have brief banks and keep an organized system of client files. Take a moment to review the client's file and any associated work product. If the litigation is in progress, look for the case's docket number and review what has already been filed (federal courts use PACER[17]—Public Access to Court Electronic Records—and many states have electronic case management (ECM) systems[18]). Find out your firm's username and password to access PACER (or the state's ECM credentials).

Now is also the time to acquaint yourself with other attorneys and legal assistants who are working on the same client's matter. Take the time to have a conversation with your colleagues to find out what your role is. As you know, cases rarely have only one issue. Your client may have many issues and you may be asked to conduct research on only one or two specific issues. It is entirely possible you will be asked to do research on issues that may or may not be raised during litigation. Find out which issues still need more

---

[15]   The Discovery and Investigation chapter will discuss how to research a judge's prior decisions to decide whether your case is likely to succeed, based on past precedent.

[16]   Lecia Kaslofsky, *Why Litigation Lawyers are Losing 10 Hours Per Week*, CLIO (Apr. 27, 2017), https://www.clio.com/blog/litigation-lawyers-losing-hours/ (discussing the results of a study by Factbox on how disorganized lawyers lose time repeating work they have already billed for). Factbox is project management software developed for litigators and integrates with CLIO.

[17]   *Individual Court Sites*, PACER, https://www.pacer.gov/psco/cgi-bin/links.pl.

[18]   *State Court Web Sites*, NATIONAL CENTER FOR STATE COURTS, https://www.ncsc.org/information-and-resources/browse-by-state/state-court-websites.aspx.

research and what research has already been completed. If your colleagues have conducted research online using Lexis Advance® or Westlaw Edge®, they can share their research folders with you to avoid duplicating effort and expense.

In law school, you may have heard your professors tell you not to be "conclusory." However, in the practice of law, it is entirely possible that your partner is looking for a yes or no answer. "Yes, our client has a valid cause of action." Keep in mind that you will need to explain your answer (do not be conclusory!). It is always a good idea to write a quick memo or issue brief to identify all of the legal resources you have relied on to support your conclusion. This will be kept in the client's file. Even if the partner never reads what you have written, you will have provided a well thought out explanation that may be useful in the future and having a memo to refer back to can save you (or someone else) from having to duplicate your efforts a couple of weeks (or months) later.

Regardless of the size of your firm or how many clients you represent, understanding the manner in which client files and research are organized will help you be successful. Organizing your research will help you and your colleagues ensure you do not miss any deadlines or duplicate any efforts, which will save both time and money. Managing your research projects will be discussed more in the next chapter.

2. What Is Your Deadline? Alternatively, How Much Time Do You Have?

Lawyers rarely have an overabundance of time to devote to any one client. Often, the client and the attorney do not have a say in the matter of how much time is available to resolve the client's case, because you may run up against statutes of limitations. It's also possible your client may come to you after ending a relationship with another lawyer and is already nearing a deadline. Maybe your client has all the time in the world, but you are representing several clients and need to manage your time appropriately. Regardless, a deadline—even a soft deadline—should be determined at the outset of your representation.

Once you determine that your client has a valid cause of action, you will also learn how much time you have, as computed by the court system and the applicable statutes and court rules. After you initiate your cause of action, the court system will likely dictate your timetable and schedule various dates for court appearances and filing deadlines. Now you need to calculate how much time you believe it will take to successfully resolve your client's issue. If you are working with another attorney on their client's legal issue, make sure you ask about deadlines and the amount of time the attorney expects you to bill/spend.

Finding out when your deadline is may be the most important question you can ask. New associates often feel overwhelmed by the amount of work they have, usually because they have not asked the assigning partner when each project is due. This uncertainty can lead to missing a court deadline if the associate failed to organize their research projects by the date they were due. There are soft deadlines, usually set by the client or assigning partner, and hard deadlines, usually set by the court. Ask questions that will give you a complete picture of the client's needs. Having a basic understanding of how much time you have will significantly decrease your anxiety as you approach legal research and may dictate what resources you can use. You may be willing to pay more money for legal research if you have less time (and vice versa).

3. How Much Money Do You Have to Spend on Research?

This brings us to the next question you should ask your firm, "Are there any restrictions on how much time I can spend conducting legal research, or are there any limitations on the resources I use?" Most law firms are concerned with the cost of legal research and whether these expenses can (or should) be passed along to their clients. For law firms that decide to bill their clients for the expenses related to their legal research, follow the *Cost Recovery "Best Practices' Rule #1: Inform Clients That They Will Be Billed the Reasonable Charges for Online Legal Research, Above and Beyond the Researching Attorney's Hourly Rate.*"[19] It is possible that your firm has a flat-rate contract with either Lexis Advance® or Westlaw Edge, or a print law library. You need to know whether you can use Lexis Advance® or Westlaw Edge on an unlimited basis, or whether your firm prefers you conduct the initial research using the firm's print collection. Alternatively, your firm may have a policy to use your state bar association's membership to Fastcase or Casemaker before accessing other fee-based research resources.[20] Other considerations include free resources, such as a nearby law library or Google Scholar. Each resource has a list of pros and cons, which is why the need to think through what you need before you get started is paramount for cost-efficient legal research. Additionally, your research options may change depending on your client.[21]

---

[19]   Although this article is more than ten years old, it does an excellent job of discussing options for recovering online legal research expenses. A survey of small law firms provides the statistics reported in the paper. Cary J. Griffith & Vicki C. Krueger, *Recovering Online Legal Research Sots: Best Practices for Enhancing Small Firm Profitability and Service to Clients* (June 2005), https://www.americanbar.org/content/dam/aba/migrated/genpractice/resources/costrecovery/WhitePaper_Cost Recovery.authcheckdam.pdf. For more current information on billing trends, see the 2018 Cost Recovery Survey (produced annually by Rob Mattern & Associates and available at https://matternassoc.com/cost-recovery/.

[20]   Jennifer L. Behrens, Associate Director for Administration & Scholarship and Senior Lecturing Fellow at Duke Law School Library, has created a map that tracks the availability of Fastcase or Casemaker legal research services available through a state bar association membership at https://law.duke.edu/lib/statebarassociations/.

[21]   At one of the law firms I worked at, we asked LexisNexis® and Westlaw to create separate research portals that provided access to primary sources only. These research portals were used primarily for our pro bono clients.

If you are working in a law firm, your firm may have restrictions on fee-based legal research. At large law firms, entering a valid client matter number is required before anyone can log on to Lexis Advance® or Westlaw Edge to ensure recovery of research expenses. A valid client matter number is required because large law firms expect to recover all costs associated with online legal research and will bill these expenses back to the client. With this in mind, make sure you ask whether you need a client matter number (or client billing code) to log on to Lexis Advance® or Westlaw Edge. Even if your law firm does not restrict your access to Lexis Advance® or Westlaw Edge, you can keep track of your research by changing the Client ID or code every time you log on and save what you find to a client's folder.

Reprinted from LexisNexis® with permission. Copyright 2019 LexisNexis®.
All rights reserved.

Reprinted from Westlaw with permission. Copyright 2019,
Thomson Reuters. All rights reserved.

If you have not determined whether your client has a valid cause of action, you may wish to begin your research using free or low-cost legal research resources instead of Lexis Advance® or Westlaw Edge (unless you have a flat-rate contract). If you spend a lot of money on research only to learn that your client *does not* have a valid cause of action, how will your firm absorb these costs?

Legal research can be expensive and it may be difficult to predict how much money you will need to spend before you have fully researched your client's issue. Think carefully about the amount of time you have, who your client is, and the cost-recovery method you plan to use.[22] The type of research you need may determine the resources you use. If you need to research an issue by the end of the day, you probably will not have time to use the free resources at the local law library.[23] If you are short on time, it may be more cost-efficient to use a fee-based legal research resource such as Bloomberg Law, Casemaker, Fastcase, Lexis Advance®, or Westlaw Edge. Although your research costs may be higher, accessing the resource from your desktop will save you time (and saves you from an afternoon of anxiety—priceless!).

---

[22] A quote from motivational speaker, Jim Rohn, seems apt, "Time is more valuable than money. You can get more money, but you cannot get more time." BRAINYQUOTE, https://www.brainyquote.com/quotes/jim_rohn_147516.

[23] Consider the amount of time it would take to jump in your car, drive to the law library, find a parking spot, conduct the research in the print resources, find money for the photocopier, return to the firm, and begin drafting your analysis.

The sad truth is that it is nearly impossible to provide quality legal research quickly and cheaply. You should weigh the following three factors before you begin every legal research project: *good*, *cheap*, and *fast*. This book will only discuss resources that are *good*, which leaves you with only one choice to make: which factor—cheap or fast—is the most important for your client (alternatively, do you have more time or more money?).

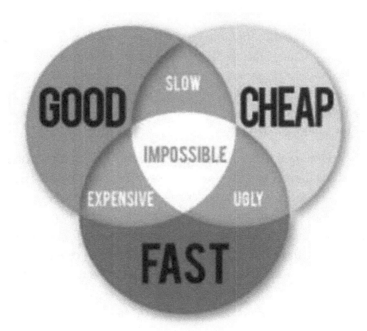

This book will help identify available *good* resources to you at each stage of the litigation process and rank them on whether they are *cheap* and/or *fast*. Identifying which factor is the most important will help narrow your options and streamline the research process based on the amount of time and money you have available. For each legal research project, you should weigh the pros and cons of the resources you have access to. This will help you determine which resource will be the best choice based on money, time, access, etc. Assuming you have access to a computer and a reliable internet connection, you will always have access to *good* free legal research resources.[24] However, it may be in your best interest to spend money on a fee-based resource, such as the many resources available through Bloomberg Law, Casemaker, Fastcase, Lexis Advance®, or Westlaw Edge.

The legal research resources I will refer to throughout this book are available online via subscriptions to Bloomberg Law, Lexis Advance®, and Westlaw Edge. I will also suggest print materials that would be a good addition to your law library from the major legal vendors. Also discussed are low-cost online legal research services, such as Casemaker and Fastcase,[25] and reliable free internet resources, such as Google Scholar. Each resource will receive a ranking in the *good, cheap*, and *fast* chart for easy reference. For those resource that are costly, but may be worth the expenditure, there will be an additional explanation of why these resources are mentioned (usually these resources offer substantial time savings).

Unfortunately, information is a valuable commodity and some fee-based services require a subscription for access.[26] Additionally, you may have a subscription to Lexis Advance® or Westlaw Edge,

---

[24] Two reliable free legal research starting points include Google Scholar, https://scholar.google.com/ (provides access to state and federal case law) and the Library of Congress, http://www.loc.gov/law/help/guide/states.php (provides a list of state and territory laws, many of which include links to unannotated versions of state statutory codes). Another free resource available to many law school graduates is the Law Journal Library collection on HeinOnline. Check with your alma mater to find out if you have access to free law reviews and journals through HeinOnline.

[25] The Tennessee Bar Association provides members with access to Fastcase as a benefit of membership, therefore, the Lincoln Memorial University (LMU) Law Library also subscribes to Fastcase for our students. I may mention Casemaker in relation to Fastcase, but any content or functionality I discuss will come from Fastcase.

[26] I consider the access to qualify information as an unfortunate impediment to justice. I encourage all fee-based services to allow non-subscribers to search their services for free and have the option to purchase documents on a per document or per hourly charge. To learn about the subscription prices for Bloomberg Law, Lexis Advance®, and Westlaw Edge, please contact your local account representative, or Google: pricing and ___ [insert the research service name] to find out your local contact.

but your subscription may limit your access to many of the secondary sources I will discuss throughout this book. If you have a subscription to Lexis Advance® or Westlaw Edge, you can usually view the price of a resource before you decide to purchase it. This book will provide you with an explanation of the resources that will most likely be "pushed" along with your primary research results and give you a better idea of when a resource is worth the investment.

For example, those resources not included in your flat-rate subscription may still be worth the additional expense. On Lexis Advance® and Westlaw Edge, searching is free, with a subscription. Both services also push relevant information to you related to your search terms, but outside of the search parameters, you have set. For example, if you limit your search to law reviews and journals only, Westlaw may push a *Causes of Action* article with your law review results, if it is on point with your search terms. How does this miracle of research happen? Through the incredible search algorithms of Lexis Advance®[27] and Westlaw Edge®[28] and artificial intelligence (AI).[29]

Legal AI is based on existing case law and related data, but computers compile and analyze information much faster than a human. The search algorithms used by Lexis Advance® and Westlaw Edge help researchers find what they need by interpreting a legal search query and adding additional synonyms or legal phrases behind the scenes. If you have ever researched an issue and found that the results provided by Lexis Advance® and/or Westlaw Edge

---

[27] Marty Kilmer & Ian Koenig, *Understanding the Technology and Search Algorithm Behind Lexis Advance*, LEXISNEXIS LAWSCHOOLS (Oct. 2013), https://www.you tube.com/watch?v=bxJzfYLwXYQ&feature=youtu.be.

[28] *WestSearch: The World's Most Advanced Legal Search Engine*, THOMSON REUTERS (2016) http://info.legalsolutions.thomsonreuters.com/pdf/wln2/l-355700_ v2.pdf.

[29] *7 Things Legal Professionals Need to Know About AI* (Infographic), https:// legal.thomsonreuters.com/en/insights/infographics/7-things-law-firms-should-know-about-legal-ai.

do not have any of the search terms you have entered, but are remarkably on point with your client's issue, you have already experienced how search algorithms work.[30]

> Think of legal research like a jigsaw puzzle, but with some added complications. You don't know the picture the completed puzzle is supposed to form, you don't know how many pieces the puzzle has, and you have to assemble the puzzle under extreme time pressure. This analogy captures the two great challenges faced by lawyers performing legal research today: they don't have enough time for the task, and they lack confidence in their results.[31]

Legal AI attempts to minimize the time and effort lawyers spend on legal research and other legal tasks. However, the "explosion of information contributes to the second major problem facing legal researchers—the crisis of confidence when it comes to the accuracy and reliability of research results."[32] The goal of this book is to help you identify research resources that will help you conduct research to find what you need during each stage of litigation. Unfortunately, neither humans nor computers are perfect, and "either working alone is inferior to the combination of both."[33]

---

[30] David Lat, *How Artificial Intelligence is Transforming Legal Research*, ABOVE THE LAW, https://abovethelaw.com/law2020/how-artificial-intelligence-is-trans forming-legal-research/ (provides an overview of legal analytics and an infographic of legal research tools. This article is sponsored by Thomson Reuters, and discusses the features of the legal analytics available on Westlaw Edge).

[31] Id.

[32] Id.

[33] Comment from Justin Brown, one of 20 corporate law attorneys involved in a study that compared the time and results of their legal expertise in spotting issues in Non-Disclosure Agreements (NDAs) contracts against the LawGeex AI. Jonathan Marciano, *20 Top Lawyers Were Beaten by Legal AI. Here Are Their Surprising Responses*, HACKER NOON (Oct. 25, 2018), https://hackernoon.com/20-top-lawyers-were-beaten-by-legal-ai-here-are-their-surprising-responses-5dafdf25554d.

Lexis Advance®, Westlaw Edge,[34] or Bloomberg Law		
GOOD	~~**CHEAP**~~	**FAST**
High quality, dependable, current, lots of value-added features, Shepard's / KeyCite / BCite, and research assistance from a lawyer is available 24/7 through chat or phone.	Fee-based, requires a contract subscription, and documents viewed in full text that are outside of the subscription can be expensive.	Desktop or access from anywhere you have an internet or Wi-Fi connection and a laptop, smart phone, iPad, etc.[35]
Print Materials **(BNA, CCH, LexisNexis®, NITA, West Publishing,** **Wolters Kluwer/Aspen, etc.)**		
GOOD **(when updated)**	**CHEAP** **(when borrowed)**	**FAST** **(when readily** **available)**
PROS: High quality and dependable. CONS: Print materials require	PROS: The investment in some print materials can be used as a capital tax deduction (books	PROS: Available in your office or firm library.

---

[34] There is a *Pricing Guidelines for Commercial Plans: Quick Reference Guide* available to our students on Westlaw that was last updated in January 2019, https://static.legalsolutions.thomsonreuters.com/static/pdf/commercial_plans_pricing.pdf.

[35] Please refer to Chapter 5: Ethics of Legal Research for a more thorough discussion about the need to take reasonable steps to prevent any unauthorized access to client information while doing research on an unsecured Wi-Fi network.

periodic updating and may be six weeks (or more) out of date on the day of receipt. Although the author and publisher may be excellent, you will always need to make sure the information you are relying on is current, creating an additional research step.	are even cheaper when used at a local law library!). CONS: Recovering the firm's investment of print resources from your clients is not an easily an explainable expense (other than photocopies).	CONS: Only one attorney can use a book at a time (a database can be used by several attorneys at the same time); the book/volume you need may be checked-out or otherwise unavailable; the book you need may require travel to a local law library, or the assistance of a law librarian, and the item may not circulate outside of the library (nearly 80% of most academic law library collections do not circulate.)
Casemaker and Fastcase[36]		
GOOD	**CHEAPer**	**FAST**
Good quality, dependable, some	Fee-based and requires a	Desktop or access from anywhere you

---

[36] Jennifer L. Behrens, Associate Director for Administration & Scholarship and Senior Lecturing Fellow at Duke Law School, created a color-coded map of the United States that shows the 49 states and the District of Columbia that offer Casemaker and/ or Fastcase (available at https://law.duke.edu/lib/statebarassociations/. The Texas state bar association offers both, while the California state bar offers neither

value-added features, and assistance available through chat or phone. The search engines are designed for lawyers, not laypeople (like Google).	subscription that is usually only a few hundred dollars *per year*. Additional content may be added for an additional fee, depending on your practice area and jurisdiction.	have an internet or Wi-Fi connection and a laptop, smart phone, iPad, etc.[37] Depending on your practice area and jurisdiction, the secondary sources and value-added features may save time.
Reliable Internet Resources **(Google Scholar, Court Web Sites, Legal Directories)**		
GOOD	**CHEAP**	**FAST**
Primary sources available from state or federal government entities; unannotated codes from commercial vendors; and free resources provided through your state bar or the ABA.	Usually available without a subscription on a per document fee (state bar association or ABA section membership may be required for access).	Desktop or access from anywhere you have an internet or Wi-Fi connection and a laptop, smart phone, iPad, etc.[38] CONS: may require more time than using Bloomberg Law, Casemaker, Fastcase, Lexis

(although city and county bars within California may offer access). Casemaker is available in 19 states; Fastcase is available in 31 states.

[37] Please refer to Chapter 5: Ethics of Legal Research about the need to take reasonable steps to prevent any unauthorized access to client information while doing research on an unsecured Wi-Fi network.

[38] Id.

		Advance®, or Westlaw Edge due to fewer value-added features and very little support or research assistance available.

a. *What Legal Research Resources Are Available?*

This book assumes all readers have access to a reasonably good computer and a reliable internet connection. With these assumptions in mind, everyone has access to Good and free legal research options. The real question becomes, Why would I pay to use Bloomberg Law, Casemaker, Fastcase, Lexis Advance®, or Westlaw Edge? There are a lot of reasons why you may choose to pay for something that is available for free in the public domain, and almost all relate to time savings. Let's consider what you cannot get for free.

Free resources do not offer any "value-added" content. Value-added content is all the extra content created by editors that make researching legal issues so much easier. Examples include:

- annotations (editorial insights on how courts distinguish applying the law to individual facts),

- hypertext or internal links to related secondary source content (such as treatises or related finding aids),

- pending laws (proposed legislation or pending regulations), and

- related primary sources.

BCite, KeyCite, and Shepard's are examples of value-added content. While free resources are great places to start, your legal analysis should never end without a thorough examination of how courts in your jurisdiction have applied a legal concept, and whether you have the most current content. There is a reason lawyers love *stare decisis.* Lawyers who want to persuade a court to rule in their favor need to provide ample authorities to support their claim. Fee-based legal research resources are often the fastest way to find what is current and authoritative, thanks to all of those value-added extras like the ability to sort your case law results by court, date, or relevancy.

While case law is available for free through Google Scholar, it will take a considerable amount of time to cull through your results. Google Scholar's algorithm is not developed for practicing attorneys like the algorithms of Lexis Advance® and Westlaw Edge.[39] Consider the amount of time trying to find what you need instead of finding what you need and then developing your legal argument. If you do not conduct adequate research, you may not be able to develop a valid argument. As Don MacLeod, the law librarian from Debevoise & Plimpton, LLP advises, be careful of the seemingly magical answers Google delivers.[40]

> Those answers might not be the right answer or the thorough answer. The ease of use also lulls researchers into asking simplistic questions that can be asked using Google syntax and not the more powerful and queries that can be created using modern legal search tools. Google is

---

[39] Susan Nevelow Mart, *The Algorithm as a Human Artifact: Implications for Legal [Re]Search,* 109 L. LIB. J. 387 (2017) (discusses algorithms and classification and compares search results from Casetext, Fastcase, Google Scholar, Lexis Advance®, Ravel, and Westlaw.)

[40] *Supra,* note 26.

a good place to start your research, but a terrible place to end it.[41]

This book attempts to provide you with the information you need to spend more time or spend more money at each stage of the litigation process. Regardless of what resource you use or how much money you spend, ultimately, your client is depending on you for legal advice on their unique situation.

4. What Are You Looking for—or What Is the Relevant Law? (*i.e.*, Statutes, Case Law, Regulations, Court Rules, etc.)

During your first year of law school, you learn about the primary sources of law and the corresponding branch of the government responsible for their creation.[42] In the United States, the Constitution dictates how the law is created and the powers of each of the three branches of government: the judiciary, the legislature, and the executive. The principle of federalism divides power between federal and state governments, and the state government structure closely mirrors that of the federal government. The legislature creates laws that are codified into statutory codes and the executive branch is charged with enforcing those laws. The judiciary has the power of review to interpret the meaning of statutes and regulations.

Throughout law school, students spend a great deal of time reading edited case law to learn how the courts have interpreted the law with differing facts. It is common for new associates to forget everything they have learned in legal research and begin all legal research projects in a case law database. While this may

---

[41] Id.

[42] If you need a quick review of primary sources, I recommend Kent Olson's PRINCIPLES OF LEGAL RESEARCH (2d ed. 2015). The first chapter provides an overview of the United States Legal System and a quick explanation of the three branches of government and the primary sources they create.

provide an answer, it is often time consuming and does not always provide the best answer. Additionally, a case that appears on point, but is outside of your jurisdiction, will only be persuasive, rather than binding, on your court. Instead of diving straight into case law for every project, consider beginning with the relevant law or regulation. Once you understand the underlying law, then you can begin to read cases with similar facts.

Here is an example of why the "case law first" approach often fails. As a law librarian, I often receive calls from local attorneys and our graduates, asking for help with research. Recently, an attorney called because they were asked to research what a "reasonable amount of time" is. The backstory involves a tenant who stopped paying rent and a landlord who issued an eviction notice. When the tenant received the eviction notice, miraculously, they started paying rent again. Several months go by and the tenant pays their rent on time, but then the tenant stops paying rent again. The attorney wants to know what a reasonable about of time is before the landlord can file another eviction notice, or if the initial notice is still in effect. The attorney began their research in a state case law database, searching for "a reasonable amount of time." Not surprisingly, the courts have not discussed what a reasonable amount of time is (because the statute is clear) and therefore, the attorney did not find the answer to their question. In this scenario, the attorney should have started by reading the landlord and tenant statutes, where they would have found:

> Except as provided in this section, fourteen (14) days' notice by a landlord shall be sufficient notice of termination of tenancy for the purpose of eviction of a residential tenant, if the tenancy is for one of the following reasons:

> A)   Tenant neglect or refusal to pay rent that is due
> and is in arrears, upon demand.[43]

Let's pause for a moment and consider how we would approach this question if a law professor was asking this question. The professor would ask, What is the issue? Then it would be the job of the law student to find the rule, or applicable law, provide some analysis of the law to the facts, and offer a conclusion. Here, we are not really looking for the definition of what a reasonable amount of time is, but an understanding of the basic tenets (if you will) of landlord and tenant law.[44]

Additionally, many states have their statutory codes available for free.[45] Using an online state statutory code, expand the table of contents to find the applicable code section. This process is easy and can quickly identify statutory sections that may apply. State statutes are usually much shorter than most court decisions, meaning there is less to read, ultimately resulting in a faster approach to finding the rule we need. In our scenario above, the caption for our statutory section is "notice of termination by landlord."[46] If your state has an annotated statute, and your statute has been interpreted by the courts, a link to the court's decision is only a click away, with no additional searching required! If you are using an unannotated code, you can find cases that have interpreted your statute by searching for the specific statutory section in a case law database.

Example: 66-7-109[47]

---

[43]   TENN. CODE. ANN. § 66-7-109(a)(1)(A) (Lexis Advance 2019).

[44]   The Uniform Residential Landlord and Tennant Act 1972 law has been adopted by 17 states.

[45]   Refer to Chapter 2: Litigation Phase I: Case Assessment and Development for more information on finding state statutory resources.

[46]   *Supra*, note 29.

[47]   TENN. CODE ANN. § 66-7-109 (Lexis Advance 2019). Practitioners do not always follow the citation suggestions of the Bluebook. If you are searching in a state case

When you begin a research project, think about what the issue is and then consider the branch of government responsible for creating your likely rule source. Statutes and regulations are not assigned or discussed in law school at the same frequency of case law, and are usually overlooked by new associates. Even when your research project requires you to understand how the law has been interpreted by the courts, I would still suggest beginning with a quick review of the applicable statutes.

There are times when your research projects are not *legal* research projects. You may need to find statistics to support your argument, or you may need to refer to authoritative, cross-disciplinary resources. If you are looking for statistics, make sure you find the original source—usually a state or federal government agency. Although associations or interested parties may cite to the official statistics, find and cite to the original source. Even when you are not referencing a source of law, you should still consider if your source is authoritative and will be persuasive to a judge.

5. How Will You Know When to Stop Researching an Issue? How Will You Know When You Have Found What You Are Looking for?

a)   When the various primary sources reference one another

b)   When you find the same primary resources, regardless of your search terms

c)   When you run out of money

d)   When you run out of time

e)   Any of the above!

---

law database, you may get better results by searching for the specific statutory codification, not the exact Bluebook citation.

The correct answer here is: e) any of the above. In a perfect world with unlimited time, money, and resources, the correct answer is a) or b), when you have found the primary sources to support your legal argument or when your research directs you to the same primary sources, regardless of your search terms. When you see the same primary sources (the same case, statutory section, etc.) referenced in all the secondary sources you read (law review articles, treatises, etc.), regardless of the search terms you use, then you can feel confident you have thoroughly researched your issue. However, it is often a deadline or a lack of funds ending a research project, which is exactly why being time and cost-efficient with legal research is so important. (Not to mention the "adequately representing your client" thing, which will be discussed at length in The Ethics of Legal Research chapter). A recent survey of state and federal judges found that in 83% of their cases, the judge or their clerks catch relevant cases that are missing from the attorneys" briefs.[48]

Good legal research skills will make the rest of your representation easier. If you are having trouble writing a brief, you may need to do more research. If you have trouble answering your client's questions, you may need to do more research. Every decision an attorney makes begins with some level of legal research. Over time, attorneys remember laws, decisions, court rules, etc., which will ultimately make the legal research process faster. Regardless, you should always update your research to verify it is still good law (by using BCite, KeyCite, or Shepard's). Every new client will introduce new facts to consider and the courts will address some of these issues. In addition, the legislature will introduce and amend new laws every year. These constant changes

---

[48] This survey may be biased, because it was conducted by Casetext. The survey results are available at https://info.casetext.com/report-prevalence-of-missing-precedents/. Bias or not, the statistics do indicate that judges are aware of missing relevant precedent in case briefs, which is a poor indicator of quality legal research skills!

in the law explain why legal research will be an ongoing task for every lawyer, regardless of practice area.

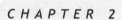

CHAPTER 2

Litigation Phase I: Case Assessment Part 1: Is There a Valid Cause of Action?

Law school prepares you for the *practice* of law through experiential courses such as Advanced Legal Research. Learning how to conduct efficient legal research will help your practice thrive. Before you go to trial, there are a zillion decisions you will need to make. First and foremost is whether your client has a valid cause of action worth pursuing. This chapter will identify the legal research resources available to help you determine whether your client has a valid cause of action. The next chapter will help you determine whether the client's cause of action is worth pursuing. Both chapters will provide suggestions on how to save time and money in the process. If you decide not to represent a client, it is unlikely they will reimburse you for any legal research expenditures, or for your time!

When you meet a potential new client for the first time, they will share their story. Your client will share facts.[1] It will be up to you to determine what the legal issues are. In law school, you learn the basics of tort or property law and learn to apply the rules you have learned to facts supplied by your professors in law school exam essays. Throughout the semester, you read edited cases that only address the issue you are studying and only discuss the applicable rule of law. However, in the real practice of law, things can get messy. Your client will likely have more than one legal issue, and they may have an issue that falls under a subject area you did not study in law school.

Before you begin research, identify your client's issue. When your client has more than one issue, identify which issue is the most time-sensitive or the most pertinent to the rest of your client's case. Categorize your issues into the general subject area—contract, tort, property—and then identify the more specific area of law. There may be issues that cross over several subject areas. For example, if a female client comes to your office believing they are a victim of employment discrimination, where should you begin?

Your client will share many details, but likely no legal concepts or legal terms of art. Your client will tell you a lot of facts, which are not legal concepts. This is where the IRAC[2] skills learned in law school will pay off. All of those outlines you created in law school will serve as a way to organize your client's facts and help you guide your client's discussion toward information you need to determine whether they have a valid cause of action. Your first step in finding any legal solution is to identify the issue. As your client shares their story, identify the broad issues and any sub issues. Once you have

---

[1]   But they may not tell you everything, or the truth. Casey C. Sullivan, *What To Do When Clients Lie*, FINDLAW (Apr. 10, 2015), https://blogs.findlaw.com/ strategist/2015/04/what-to-do-when-clients-lie.html.

[2]   Issue, Rule, Analysis, and Conclusion. Other acronyms may be used, but for legal research, you must first identify the issue and then find the associated rules applicable to your jurisdiction.

identified the legal issue(s), you can start asking your client to provide facts to support or negate the elements necessary to establish a prima facie case.

1. Does Your Client Have a Valid Cause of Action?

Let's begin with a quick refresher and find out how *Black's Law Dictionary*[3] defines what a "cause of action" is:

cause of action (15c) **1.** A group of operative facts giving rise to one or more bases for suing; a factual situation that entitles one person to obtain a remedy in court from another person; after the crash, Aronson had a cause of action.

> What is a cause of action? Jurists have found it difficult to give a proper definition. It may be defined generally to be a situation or state of facts that entitles a party to maintain an action in a judicial tribunal. This state of facts may be—(*a*) a primary right of the plaintiff actually violated by the defendant; or (*b*) the threatened violation of such right, which violation the plaintiff is entitled to restrain or prevent, as in case of actions or suits for injunction; or (*c*) it may be that there are doubts as to some duty or right, or the right beclouded by some apparent adverse right or claim, which the plaintiff is entitled to have cleared up, that he may safely perform his duty, or enjoy his property. Edwin E. Bryant, *The Law of Pleading Under the Codes of Civil Procedure* 170 (2d ed. 1899).[4]

---

[3] All law students should own a legal dictionary. *Black's Law Dictionary* is currently in the tenth edition, published by Thomson Reuters, and available on Westlaw Edge. *Ballentine's Law Dictionary* is currently in the third edition, published by LexisNexis, and available on Lexis Advance®. If you do not already own a law dictionary in print, ask for one for graduation. Legal dictionaries are not terribly expensive and you will use it over and over again.

[4] *Cause of Action,* BLACK'S LAW DICTIONARY (11th ed. 2019).

Now that we are all on the same page, it is clear why knowing whether your client has a *valid* cause of action is a necessary first step in your research. The sad reality of the practice of law is not all wrongs are legal wrongs, and not all injured clients can recover satisfactorily through the judicial system.

Additionally, your client may have a legal issue that does not fall under the broad subjects you studied in law school, leaving you with a lot of questions on where to begin. If you cannot identify what the legal issue is, where should you begin? When you are a solo practitioner, or in a small practice, you may not have a colleague to turn to with questions. This is where your legal research skills will pay off. Not only will legal research help you identify the rules that govern your client's legal issue, but the process of legal research will also help you understand how those rules apply to your client's unique circumstances. The goal of legal research is twofold: first, research the legal issue, then read what you have found to further your understanding. As a new attorney, you may find that you need to teach yourself an area of law that you did not study in law school.[5] This is why you should consider starting your research with secondary sources, which are intended to be read and are written to explain complex legal issues.[6]

a. *Secondary Sources—Treatises & Law Reviews*

If you have access to a legal research service, begin by browsing through the available subjects or practice areas for treatises on point with your client's issue.[7] This will not take a lot

---

[5]   For example, bitcoin and cryptocurrencies are new areas of law that most practicing attorneys never had a chance to study in law school.

[6]   Secondary sources are any sources that interpret the law, but are not created by one of the three branches of government. Secondary sources include law review articles, treatises, books, etc.

[7]   Law libraries catalog the materials they own through a service called OCLC WorldCat. Originally, OCLC was an acronym for the Ohio Consortium of Library Catalogs, but the service has grown to include library catalog records from around the world, hence the addition of WorldCat to the name. To find a law library with resources near you, go to http://www.worldcat.org/ and follow the link to "Find a

of time, and there is no cost for browsing through sources (unless your subscription contract is by the minute/hour). Bloomberg Law, Fastcase, Lexis Advance®, and Westlaw Edge all provide a wealth of secondary sources, only available through that particular research service. For every legal issue, there is usually a legal expert somewhere who has not only had an issue similar to your client's, but represented several clients with similar issues and has become somewhat of an expert in representing these types of clients. These lawyers are also known as "authors" because they often write treatises or law review articles on the issues they are most experienced with. A treatise will provide an overview of the subject and include relevant cases and statutes. Treatises can be specific to one state's jurisdiction, or cover the issue nationwide.[8] PRINCIPLES OF LEGAL RESEARCH, 2d provides a good review of what treatises are:

> These are scholarly surveys providing exhaustive coverage of particular fields of law. A treatise is similar to an encyclopedia in that it methodically outlines the basic aspects of legal doctrine, but is focused on a specific subject usually giving a treatise greater depth and insight.

> The traditional treatise is a multi-volume work covering a broad area of legal doctrine such as contracts or trusts.10 Modern treatises tend to focus on increasingly narrow areas of law, and many are just one or two volumes. Treatises are published in bound volumes or looseleaf

---

Library." You can search by zip code and then browse through a list of participating libraries near you. If you are looking for an academic law library, make sure your look for the link to the law school's catalog, not the main university's library. The law school library usually catalogs their materials separately from the main university's holdings. When you have found the law library you need, search their library catalog for resources that may be useful to your practice. Most academic law libraries, both public and private, are open to state bar members, but not all materials circulate. Check with your law library's policies, usually available on their website.

[8]   Another West Academic title, Kent C. Olson's, PRINCIPLES OF LEGAL RESEARCH (2nd 2015), includes a list of Treatises and Services By Subject in the appendix. The appendix also includes law library call numbers, if you are close to an academic law library.

binders, and are generally updated annually with either pocket parts or looseleaf supplements.

Treatises are the texts most likely to be available through one of the major online services, although some are still available only in print. When using a treatise in any format, you should be aware of how current it is and look for more recent authority as necessary. In print, check the date of the most recent edition or supplement; online, look for an information icon or "Currency" link.[9]

If you cannot find, or do not have access to a treatise on point with your issue, look for a law review or law journal article.

The terms "law journal" and "law review" in periodical names do not have distinct meanings. Many legal newspapers are called "journals," as in the *National Law Journal* or the *New York Law Journal*, but the name is also used by prestigious academic law reviews such as the *Yale Law Journal*. Some journals, such as Constitutional Commentary or Health Matrix, use neither term in their titles but are nonetheless academic law reviews. It is a periodical's form and content that determine its nature, not its title.[10]

Many law schools offer their graduates free access to HeinOnline's Law Journal Library.[11] From the HeinOnline website, the Law Journal Library collection contains:

> more than 2,600 law and law-related periodicals. Subjects covered include criminal justice, political science, technology, human rights, and more. Coverage

---

[9]   KENT C. OLSON, PRINCIPLES OF LEGAL RESEARCH (2nd ed. 2015). Also included in this book is an Appendix of Treatises and Services by Subject.

[10]   Id. at 340.

[11]   *Law Journal Library*, HEINONLINE, https://home.heinonline.org/content/law-journal-library/.

LITIGATION PHASE I: CASE ASSESSMENT PART 1:
IS THERE A VALID CAUSE OF ACTION?

35

for all journals is from inception and goes through the
most currently published issues allowed based on
contracts with publishers. About 90% of journals are
available through the current issue or volume. Search by
article title, author, subject, state or country published,
full text, and narrow by date.[12]

Check with your alma matter to find out if they provide their
graduates with access.[13] If you do not have access to the HeinOnline
Law Journal Library, law review articles can also be found using
Google Scholar. Law reviews and journals will often begin with an
overview of an issue, or provide the history of a legal concept, which
makes them an excellent place to being your research.

b. *Legal Encyclopedias, Jurisprudences, & Wikipedia*

There will be times when your client has an issue that may
require a quick refresher or initially appears straightforward, but
you may later discover is fairly complex. For example, if your client
believes they have an employment discrimination claim, you may be
wondering which law will apply. We know our client is a female, if
our client is also over the age of 40, other employment
discrimination laws may also apply. When you do not know where to
begin researching your client's issue, begin with a legal
encyclopedia or jurisprudence. There are two national legal
encyclopedias, *Corpus Juris Secundum*[14] (C.J.S.) and *American*

---

[12] Id.

[13] 40 academic law libraries provide their graduates with access, including the
Lincoln Memorial University Duncan School of Law, the University of Tennessee, and
Vanderbilt.

[14] From the scope information on Westlaw, "Cited and quoted as authority in
courtrooms across the country, *C.J.S.*, a national legal encyclopedia, covers state and
federal legal topics from A to Z. General rules of law are summarized in blackletter
law headings and expanded upon in the text. The book also provides the limitations
and exceptions to the rules where appropriate. Since the citations and the supporting
cases involve both state and federal courts, the user gets a full perspective of the law
in a local jurisdiction as well as across the country."

Jurisprudence, 2d (Am. Jur. 2d).[15] Both provide explanations and references to court cases across the nation. Am. Jur. 2d is available on both Westlaw Edge and Lexis Advance®, but C.J.S. is available only on Westlaw. Both are also available in print in most academic and court law library collections. Additionally, most states provide a state-specific legal encyclopedia or jurisprudence, which will focus on how courts have decided legal issues within that particular jurisdiction.[16] Although legal encyclopedias primarily provide researchers with related case law, they may also identify state and federal statutes.

While you are in law school and have access to a plethora of research services, use all of them! Our employment discrimination example above is illustrative on how two different legal encyclopedias (originally created with different editors employed by different companies[17]) treat the same issue slightly differently. Beginning with the Westlaw version of Am. Jur. 2d, search for **"employment discrimination"**.[18] When you receive a large number of results,[19] the issue you are searching for is too broad and needs

---

[15]   From the source information on Lexis Advance®, "American Jurisprudence, Second Edition, published by West Publishing Company a division of Thomson Reuters, is an encyclopedic text of both procedural and substantive American law, state, federal, criminal, civil and procedural. Consisting of over 430 topic headings (titles), Am. Jur. 2d articles collect, examine, and summarize the broad principles of American law and, at the same time, provide direct leads to supporting cases, related annotations, forms, proofs, and trial techniques."

[16]   For example, the TENNESSEE JURISPRUDENCE is published by Matthew Bender & Company, Inc., and available on Lexis Advance®. From the Lexis Advance® source description note, "Tennessee Jurisprudence offers encyclopedic treatment of the civil and criminal law of Tennessee. It analyzes the state's case law, statutes, rules, and regulations, and offers extensive references to other publications to save you valuable research time."

[17]   CORPUS JURIS SECUNDUM has always been published by West (now owned by Thomson Reuters). The AMERICAN JURISPRUDENCE, however, was originally published by Lawyers Co-operative Publishing Company. In 1989, International Thomson (now Thomson Reuters) acquired Lawyers Co-op. Today, both are published by the same company,

[18]   Always put quotation marks around phrases to keep the words in the same order. On Westlaw Edge, a space is interpreted as an implied OR. On Lexis Advance®, a space is interpreted as an implied AND. Entering **employment discrimination** in the Westlaw Am. Jur. 2d database returns 3,989 hits (employment OR discrimination).

[19]   The first search returned 775 results.

a more narrow focus. Change your search terms to **"employment discrimination" /s female**[20] to reduce your search results to a more manageable number.

Reprinted from Westlaw with permission. Copyright 2019,
Thomson Reuters. All rights reserved.

Selecting the second result, § 1118 Generally, provides us with more information on the legal issue.

---

[20] The second search returned five results. Adding /s to the phrase narrows the results to those results that include female within the same sentence as the phrase, employment discrimination. Select the ADVANCED search option to see more proximity operators, connectors and expanders to help improve search accuracy.

Reprinted from Westlaw with permission. Copyright 2019, Thomson Reuters. All rights reserved.

The screenshot above provides a clear example of how a legal encyclopedia can provide a quick answer and lead you to the next step in your legal research process. Here, you learn the additional facts you need to get from your client and the first steps of the litigation process—filing a charge with the Equal Employment Opportunity Commission (EEOC).[21] The encyclopedia entry also leads you to related research resources on point with your issue, such as an *Am. Jur. Trials* entry on employment discrimination.[22] The remainder of this entry provides case annotations and on the left, additional entries will provide more explanations and court decisions on the related legal concepts.

Now let's compare similar results from *Corpus Juris Secundum* (C.J.S), beginning with the same search, **"employment discrimination" /s female**.

---

[21] 45B AM. JUR. 2D *Job Discrimination* § 1118 (Nov. 2018).

[22] 21 AM. JUR. TRIALS 1 *Emp't Discrimination Action Under Fed. Civil Rights Acts* (Nov. 2018).

Reprinted from Westlaw with permission. Copyright 2019,
Thomson Reuters. All rights reserved.

Following the link to the first entry, "bona fide occupational qualifications" provides us with another set of questions to ask our client we may not have known to consider before doing a bit of research.

Reprinted from Westlaw with permission. Copyright 2019,
Thomson Reuters. All rights reserved.

The examples above illustrate how quickly a researcher can find either an answer or a research starting point using either *Am. Jur. 2d* or *C.J.S.* Legal encyclopedias are a great first step in the legal research process and will lead researchers to authoritative resources to help resolve a client's legal issue. It is important that the researcher understand the legal issue *before* delving into case law research to save both time and money. If you didn't know about bona fide occupational qualifications, how would you know to search for them? Additionally, legal encyclopedias will provide citations to cases that have discussed the issue stated in the encyclopedia entry.

If we compare the ease of using a legal encyclopedia with the results from Google, or even Wikipedia, it will become apparent how these two free options will require a lot more time. According to Google, the web is made up of more than 60 trillion individual pages and growing.[23] Sorting through this much data to find the information you need requires using either a Search Engine or a Directory. Web Robots (or Spiders) create Search Engines, while humans create or curate topical Directories. The four most popular Search Engines are Google, Bing, Ask, or Yahoo!, but all of these Search Engines are designed to find general, not legal, information. When you are looking for legal information, you will find better search results in less time by using a Directory designed explicitly for legal research.[24] Reliable resources are LII (Cornel's Legal

---

[23] *How Search Works: From Algorithms to Answers. Google Inside Search*, https://www.google.com/insidesearch/howsearchworks/thestory.

[24] For faster and better results, use a Search Engine tailored to your research need. Google offers several Search Engines dedicated to indexing specific types of information. If you are looking for a law review article, begin your research with Google Scholar. If you are looking for news stories, begin with Google News. Marziah Karch, *10 of Google's Other Search Engines*, LIFEWIRE (Oct. 26, 2018), https://www.lifewire.com/other-search-engines-4039631.

LITIGATION PHASE I: CASE ASSESSMENT PART 1:
IS THERE A VALID CAUSE OF ACTION?

41

Information Institute),[25] Justia,[26] FindLaw,[27] and Lexis® Web.[28] Google Scholar[29] is also an option, but may require additional time to sort through the volume of non-law related results.

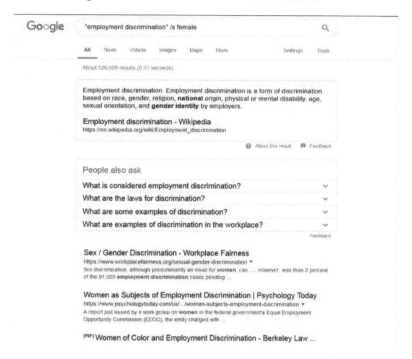

The above screen shot is from a Google search using the same narrow search we used in the legal encyclopedias, but provides us

---

[25] Legal Information Institute, https://www.law.cornell.edu/. Provides state and federal primary sources and a free legal encyclopedia called Wex.

[26] Justia, https://www.justia.com/. Provides state and federal primary law, free legal practice area resources and newsletters.

[27] FindLaw, https://www.findlaw.com/. A product of Thomson Reuters, provides state and federal primary law and forums where pro se patrons can ask questions about a legal issue, find a lawyer, and learn about the law. Also available are legal forms and newsletters.

[28] A product of LexisNexis, LexisWeb offers "all legal content. . .all sites validated" https://lexisweb.com/.

[29] Google Scholar, https://scholar.google.com/. Search for scholarly articles, including law reviews and journals, and federal and state case law. Some articles require a password or subscription for access to the full text.

with about a million results.[30] Although the first few results include a Wikipedia definition that appears useful, the Wikipedia entry is actually for the broad topic of employment discrimination and provides us with sociological information, not legal information. The second Google suggested question link, "what are the laws for discrimination?' stems from Google's AI and refers us to a free legal encyclopedia called "Wex" which is hosted by Cornell's Legal Information Institute. Following that link leads us to an entry on the broad topic of employment discrimination.

Support Us!

Legal Information Institute [LII]
OPEN ACCESS TO LAW SINCE 1992

ABOUT LII ⟩   GET THE LAW ⟩   LAWYER DIRECTORY   LEGAL ENCYCLOPEDIA ⟩   HELP OUT ⟩

ALL PAGES ARTICLES ESPAÑOL INBOX PROJECT SEARCH FAQ

Employment Discrimination

Employment Discrimination Overview:

Employment Discrimination laws seek to prevent discrimination based on race, sex, sexual orientation, religion, national origin, physical disability, and age by employers. Discriminatory practices include bias in hiring, promotion, job assignment, termination, compensation, retaliation, and various types of harassment. The main body of employment discrimination laws consists of federal and state statutes. The United States Constitution and some state constitutions provide additional protection when the employer is a governmental body or the government has taken significant steps to foster the discriminatory practice of the employer.

The Fifth and Fourteenth Amendments of the United States Constitution limit the power of the federal and state governments to discriminate. The Fifth Amendment has an explicit requirement that the federal government not deprive individuals of "life, liberty, or property" without due process of the law. It also contains an implicit guarantee that each person receive equal protection of the laws. The Fourteenth Amendment explicitly prohibits states from violating an individual's rights to due process and equal protection. In the employment context, the right of equal protection limits the power of the state and federal governments to discriminate in their employment practices by treating employees, former employees, or job applicants unequally because of membership in a group (such as a race or sex). Due process protection requires that employees receive a fair process before termination if the termination relates to a "liberty" (such as the right to free speech) or property interest. State constitutions may also afford protection from employment discrimination.

The Constitution does not directly constrain discrimination in the private sector, but the private sector has become subject to a growing body of federal and state statutes.

Federal Employment Statutes Prohibiting Discrimination

In 1963 Congress passed the Equal Pay Act, which amended the Fair Labor Standards Act. The Equal Pay Act prohibits employers and unions from paying different wages based on the employee's sex. It does not prohibit other discriminatory hiring practices. It provides that if workers perform equal work in jobs requiring "equal skill, effort, and responsibility . . .

When you begin your search with Google you need to be super-vigilant while culling through the results. Google is not designed for

---

[30]   Your results may vary. Google results include more than 200 ranking factors, such as search history, geolocation, and so much more! Brian Dean, *Google's 200 Ranking Factors: The Complete List 2018*, BACKLINKO (May 16, 2018), https://back linko.com/google-ranking-factors.

legal research like Bloomberg Law, Casemaker,[31] Fastcase, Lexis Advance®, or Westlaw Edge, which are all designed for and supported by attorneys. Even the free Wex legal encyclopedia entry is going to require a lot more work on your end. It begins with a discussion of the United States Constitution, the Fourteenth Amendment, and then rambles on to the Equal Pay Act and the Fair Labor Standards Act.[32] It would take quite a bit more time to read, learn, and ultimately glean anything useful to our fact pattern. For the same investment in the time it takes to type a search query, the entries found in *Am. Jur. 2d* and *C.J.S.* provide specific statutes, case annotations, and guidance on additional facts and next steps in the litigation process. Although the legal encyclopedia entries may incur a cost upfront (if they are not included in your flat-rate plan), the amount of time you will save by finding an entry on point with your legal issue will result in a better return on your investment (ROI).[33]

In addition, Google cannot discern between "fake" news and real news.[34] Fake news can be misleading and confusing and has the mischievous goal of deliberately attempting to mislead the reader with content appearing to be truthful.[35] Unfortunately, the popular

---

[31] Casemaker recently released a new platform, Casemaker4, which includes autofill in the search box and "intelligent algorithms to suggest related primary and secondary materials". Jean O'Grady, Casemaker Releases Casemaker4 With "Intelligent Algorithms" and New Features, DEWEY B STRATEGIC (Jun. 3, 2019), https://www.deweybstrategic.com/2019/06/casemaker-releases-casemaker4-with-intelligent-algorithms-and-new-features.html?utm_source=feedburner&utm_medium=feed&utm_campaign=Feed%3A+DeweyBStrategic+-Dewey+B+Strategic.

[32] *Employment Discrimination*, LEGAL INFO. INST., https://www.law.cornell.edu/wex/employment_discrimination.

[33] *Defining ROI Law Library Best Practices*, AM. ASSOC. L. LIBRARIES (2016), https://www.aallnet.org/wp-content/uploads/2016/01/AALL-ROI-Whitepaper-2016_FINAL.pdf.

[34] Clara Hendrickson & William A. Galston, *Big Tech Threats: Making Sense of the Backlash Against Online Platforms*, BROOKINGS (May 28, 2019), https://www.brookings.edu/research/big-tech-threats-making-sense-of-the-backlash-against-online-platforms/ (explaining how inaccurate information spawned from bad technology can disrupt democracy).

[35] Many thanks to law librarians Carol Watson, Director of the Law Library at the University of Georgia; Kristina L. Niedringhaus, Associate Dean of Library and Information Services and Associate Professor of Law at Georgia State University

appeal of the stories lure folks to read the articles and share fake news through their social media accounts, such as Facebook.[36] Moreover, the results from a Google search are displayed by numerous ranking criteria, one of which is how often a search query similar to yours has identified results that other people believe are on point with their research. However, most people are not lawyers and Google is not designed for legal research. The influx of fake news could potentially skew your top results.

Our court system applies the law to specific facts. Authoritative news sources report on facts and verify the facts they report on.[37] This is one more reason to rely on a legal research service, such as Bloomberg Law, Casemaker, Fastcase, Lexis Advance®, or Westlaw Edge for legal research, instead of a popular search engine, such as Google, which may distort or confuse the facts.[38] Besides, there is a Google-esque search box on the home page of all major legal research services and the algorithms will attempt to match search terms to related legal content, which will ultimately lead you to the law much faster than Google.

SECONDARY SOURCES		
GOOD!	CHEAP	FAST
Law Review articles	Available on all legal research	Use the Articles option on Google

---

College of Law; and Caroline Osborne, Director of the Law Library and Associate Professor of Law at West Virginia University College of Law for their PowerPoint presentation at the Southeastern Association of Law Libraries (SEAALL) Annual Meeting in 2018.

[36] From the above SEAALL presentation, in 2017, two-thirds of American adults got their news from social media.

[37] Richard W. Stevenson, *How We Fact-Check in an Age of Misinformation*, NY TIMES (Jul. 30, 2019), https://www.nytimes.com/2019/07/30/reader-center/fact-checking-politics-presidential-election.html.

[38] Additionally, Lexis Advance® will remove duplicate news articles that have been picked up by the Associated Press and republished in newspapers throughout the country.

	services. Often available for free through the law school's website.	Scholar to find a law review on your subject.
GOOD!	~~**CHEAP**~~	**FAST!** *Time saver*
Treatises	Usually available for a fee online though a legal research service, or in print. Academic and court law libraries often have a wealth of treatises that you can peruse for free.	Treatises provide a "one stop shop" on your subject, by including primary law, practice advice, forms and other related resources. Look for an index section or volume to locate what you need. Pay attention to how current the material is by looking at the date at the bottom of the page (if it's a loose-leaf treatise), the front of the first volume of a set, or the first page of the pocket part filed at the back of a volume (content may be updated bi-weekly, monthly, or annually).

GOOD	CHEAP	FAST
Encyclopedias, Jurisprudences, and Wikis	Usually available for a fee online though a legal research service, or in print. Academic and court law libraries often have at least one nationwide encyclopedia in print in addition to the state's encyclopedia/ jurisprudence.	Print sets are updated annually with pocket parts inserted in the back of each volume. Soft-bound supplements may also update the content and are shelved at the end of the set.

c. *Causes of Action, 2d*

However, one of my favorite resources to use as a starting point for legal research is not a treatise or a law review, but an aptly named set called *Causes of Action* (COA).[39] "Each article leads the practitioner through the steps necessary to determine whether particular facts give rise to a cause of action. The article analyzes the elements of the cause of action and then explains how these elements can be proved."[40] The articles begin with what is necessary to establish a prima facie case, the defenses and exceptions, and explains who can sue and who may be liable. If you have the good fortune to find a *Causes of Action* article or case

---

[39] *West's Causes of Action* (second edition, COA 2d) is published by Thomson Reuters and available on Westlaw. There are more than 70 volumes in this set. Each volume contains numerous articles and case studies on different types of actions, "including personal injury, products liability, employment, insurance, business, and many others." Please visit the Thomson Reuters website for more information at http://legalsolutions.thomsonreuters.com/law-products/Treatises/Causes-of-Action-2d/p/100028213.

[40] Preface from the print volume 66 COA 2d. (March 2015).

LITIGATION PHASE I: CASE ASSESSMENT PART 1:
IS THERE A VALID CAUSE OF ACTION?

47

summary on your issue, you have just saved yourself a lot of time, which would otherwise be spent conducting more research. *Causes of Action* is available in print (now in the second edition) and also online via Westlaw.

When you can find a law review article on point with your client's legal issue, you have a great starting point with numerous citations to related statutes, cases, etc. What makes a COA article stand out is the depth of coverage on an issue and the focus on preparing for litigation. Each COA article provides a Substantive Law Overview that includes what you need to know in order to establish a prima facie case. If you have a choice between purchasing a law review article or a COA article, consider what is included in a COA article.[41] Depending on your issue, an article will likely include a discussion of the relevant potential defenses and the parties who may be liable, in addition to all related primary sources. An example of a *Causes of Action* article useful in helping our client who believes she has an employment discrimination claim is titled, *Cause of Action Under Title VII of Civil Rights Act Against Employer for Disparate Treatment Discrimination Against Female Employee on Basis of Sex or Gender*.[42] The article identifies the scope of the Act, who may be liable and, most importantly for a new attorney, provides a checklist of information necessary to successfully represent your client.[43] When you do not have an outline or a colleague to turn to for help, look for a secondary source written by an attorney who is an expert in the field you are researching. A

---

[41] I am confident that everyone who attends or has graduated from law school is familiar with what a law review article will likely contain. If you have a subscription to Westlaw, access to a law review article outside of your plan will cost the same amount as a *Causes of Action* article, or $102. If you have found a law review article that looks good, great! If you find a law review article and a *Causes of Action* article and cannot decide between the two, I would recommend choosing the COA article because it will provide you with more thorough coverage and with more resources to continue your research.

[42] Elizabeth O'Connor Tomlinson, *Cause of Action Under Title VII of Civil Rights Act Against Employer for Disparate Treatment Discrimination Against Female Employee on Basis of Sex or Gender*, 83 CAUSES OF ACTION 2D 133 (2018).

[43] Id.

Causes of Action article discusses an issue's litigation path, from discovery to appeal. More importantly, a COA article examines the strategies necessary for both the plaintiff *and* the defendant. Finding a COA article on point with your issue is the next best thing to having an experienced mentor.

Reprinted from Westlaw with permission. Copyright 2019, Thomson Reuters. All rights reserved.

CAUSES OF ACTION, 2D		
GOOD!	~~CHEAP~~	*FAST* *time saver!*
"Causes of Action is an extensive reference collection that provides articles and case studies focusing on different types of actions, including personal injury, products liability, employment, insurance, business, and many others. Each article or case study identifies the various elements of each case, educating you on the litigation issues by offering a substantive law overview. To aid in research, the publication lists each article's coverage and includes an index of key terms and phrases. Readers	Available via Westlaw, but may not be included in subscriber plans. Available from academic law libraries; probably not available in most court, public, or law firm law libraries. Many law libraries will not circulate these volumes, which means an article would need to be photocopied, which will require additional time. Some articles can be more than 100 pages in length, making photocopy charges seem expensive. Each COA article will include the	Available via Westlaw, but may not be included in subscriber plans. Available from academic law libraries; probably not available in most court, public, or law firm law libraries. Many law libraries will not circulate these volumes, which means an article would need to be photocopied, which will require additional time (and a lot of spare change!). Each COA article will include the major primary sources of law applicable to each

will also benefit from detailed research and procedure guidelines, as well as a damages awards survey, helping you value cases from various jurisdictions." - *Scope note from Westlaw*	major primary sources of law applicable to each article topic. This will save a tremendous amount of time and primary sources can be obtained for free or at low-cost through online subscription services.	article topic. This will save a tremendous amount of time and primary sources can be obtained for free or at low-cost through online subscription services.

Despite not being Cheap, if you do have a Westlaw subscription, and a COA article title is pushed with your results, it may be well worth the per document view investment. This is why: this one resource is a one-stop shop. The article will cite to related statutes, case law, regulations AND provide a nice narrative on how everything fits together. COA articles have an article outline, which makes it super easy to find exactly what you need and may introduce additional research terms you may not have thought of. The statutes and case law cited in the article can be located through any fee-based online service or from free, reliable Internet sources. Sometimes you need to spend some money to save some time, and this is one example of a resource that will do just that.

If you cannot find a secondary source on your topic, switch gears to primary sources. Before you agree to represent any client, you need to find out what the law is and whether your client's actions are within the scope of the law, or in violation of the law. In a common law jurisdiction, the "law" may be found in case law, statutes, or regulations. You will need to thoroughly research all related primary sources to fully understand the law that applies to your client's issue.

d. *Primary Sources—Statutes*

One of the common legal research mistakes new associates make is in assuming every legal issue has already been litigated, and therefore, all legal research projects should begin with the appropriate case law database. Case law databases are huge, meaning you will need to cull through a lot of content to find what you need.[44] Depending on your issue, this can make legal research take more time than necessary. Additionally, law students tend to focus on researching the facts of a case, instead of researching legal concepts. While beginning research in a case law database is not an entirely bad approach, it may be a better idea to begin your research in the applicable state or federal statutes. Besides, statutes are mandatory authority and override any individual court decision.[45]

Instead of doing a keyword search, it is usually faster to browse through statute titles and chapters by expanding the table of contents. Once you find the applicable statute, you can find cases that have cited directly to your statutory section. In order to find state or federal statutes, first identify the issue, then which title of the law you are looking for will likely be codified.[46] This is not

---

[44] Think back to your law school library and all of those beige reporter volumes. While only 2% of cases are published, case reporters grow faster than any other set in a law library. Federal district court decisions are the most prolific, with approximately 13.5 feet of linear shelf space required each year! Thanks to Carol Collins, Head of Technical Services/Associate Professor at the University of Tennessee College of Law Library, for this information.

[45] However, the United States Supreme Court interprets constitutional challenges and the U.S. Constitution determines the lawmaking power of federal legislative, executive, and judicial branches. Likewise, state supreme courts have the same power at the state level. Usually, state and federal supreme courts try not to make decisions on issues that are the legislature's bailiwick.

[46] State and federal legislatures publish session laws chronologically. Commercial vendors later codify all of the current laws for a specific jurisdiction by subject area to make finding them easier. Commercial vendors may add additional language or cross-references to help organize the law and make it easier to read.

always easy—the statute may be codified in a specific code, like the tax code or the family code, or organized in a title you may initially overlook. However, browsing the table of contents of state and federal statutes is something you can do without incurring additional charges, either with your fee-based subscription service or using a low-cost or free internet resource. Begin by browsing through the table of contents instead of keyword searching because statutes are written with broad terms, not the specific terms from your client's facts. Most fee-based services do not charge for browsing or searching, unless you have an hourly subscription contract. You will incur charges when you "deliver" the full text of a document (view, download, email, or print).[47]

As an added bonus, beginning your research with statutes will help identify the terms the legislature has used. For example, if the police confiscated your client's truck, and your client wants his truck back, you probably want to use a search term other than "truck." The legislature writes laws intended to apply to the masses, so begin thinking about what broader category trucks (or whatever you are looking for) might be categorized under. The legislature probably did not write a law that would apply only to trucks, but it may have written a law that applies to automobiles, vehicles, personal property, or chattel. The judiciary has the power of review and will do their best to apply the vague or ambiguous laws written by legislators to an individual set of facts. When you are crafting your search query, think of synonymous terms analogous to what you are searching for.[48] If you find decisions discussing the

---

Chapter or section headings are not usually part of the binding statutory language and therefore, differences in the codification of statutes may occur when comparing two "identical" statutes from two different commercial vendors. Only the actual statutory language—not the title, chapter, or section headings—is binding law.

[47] Both Lexis Advance® and Westlaw Edge have folders where you can save the results of your research. Get in the habit of creating folders for your clients and save everything. Additionally, you can share your research, or the contents of a folder, with other members of your firm.

[48] Unlike case law databases, statute databases do not currently have the added benefit of artificial intelligence to help identify synonymous terms in the background.

seizure of a vehicle, those decisions may also apply to a confiscated truck. If you begin your search in case law, you hope the keywords you use in your search will also be used in the language of a court's decision. You may spend a lot of time reading case law trying to find your terms, rather than educating yourself on the terms used in the statute.[49] This is where legal AI can help if you are using a legal research service. The algorithms built in to the search engines of Bloomberg Law, Fastcase, Lexis Advance®, and Westlaw Edge will identify synonymous terms and incorporate those terms into your search results.

Annotated State & Federal Statutes (in print or available on Lexis Advance® or Westlaw Edge)		
GOOD	~~**CHEAP**~~	*FAST*
Good quality, updated, support available from the publisher.	Cost varies by state, but the frequency of use may justify the expense.[50]	PRINT: On your bookshelf in your office or down the

---

[49] You may search for "doctor" but the legislators used "physician." The Lexis Advance® and Westlaw Edge algorithms will add synonymous terms to your query automatically in an attempt to improve your search results. Google Scholar and other free government websites do not have sophisticated legal AI in their algorithms.

[50] Most libraries purchase the entire set, but individual volumes may also be available for purchase. Also, the "official" version of the state code is usually cheaper than the unofficial version. (Here, "official" means which commercial vendor a State has selected to publish their state code.) The following is a sample of the initial costs of a state code set and annual update from Kendall F. Svengalis's LEGAL INFORMATION BUYER'S GUIDE & REFERENCE MANUAL (2018). DEERING'S CALIFORNIA CODES ANNOTATED (LexisNexis®) is $4,444 with an annual update cost of $3,300; THE OFFICIAL CODE OF GEORGIA ANNOTATED (LEXISNEXIS®) is $395 with an annual update cost of $395; and VERNON'S ANNOTATED MISSOURI STATUTES (Thomson West) is $6,959 with an annual update cost of $5,654.

There is also a difference in price between the official and unofficial statute's costs. For example, in Tennessee, the TENNESSEE CODE ANNOTATED is the official State code, published by LexisNexis®, and available for $365 per year (both the initial and the annual update cost). The unofficial state code is published by Thomson West, WEST'S TENNESSEE CODE ANNOTATED, and is $1,649 for the initial purchase price with an annual update cost of $1,572. If you decide to purchase print materials for your collection, cost is only one factor. You should also consider how often the material is

Official and unofficial state codes are published by the state, LexisNexis®, or Thomson Reuters. Annotated! Online resources also include Shepard's or KeyCite signals for legislative alerts, hypertext links to citing court decisions, and additional annotations to research references. Westlaw Edge now includes a Compare Versions feature that displays superseded and current language, making it easier to identify how a	Your state's annotated statutes will be part of the core collection of an academic law library. Annotated codes are also available at court libraries and some public libraries (however, you will need to verify that the set is current). State statutes are updated at least once a year by pocket part (look at the back of any volume—the date the pocket part was printed will be on the cover of the pocket part). Additional updates are in softbound supplements,	hall in your firm's library = fast. Travel to a local law library = not so fast. ONLINE: Desktop access requires a subscription. Access from anywhere you have an internet or Wi-Fi connection and a laptop, smart phone, iPad, mobile device, etc.

updated, and how the material relates to the rest of the titles in your collection. This can be a lot to consider, so again, I suggest that you turn to an expert. Ken Svengalis has been keeping track of legal information costs for 25 years. His book is probably in the reference section of any academic law library, or you can purchase your own copy for a mere $189. Visit the publisher's website at http://www.nelawpress.com for more information.

statutory section has been amended or changed.	usually shelved at the end of the set.	

Casemaker and Fastcase		
GOOD	**CHEAPer**	**FAST**
Good quality, dependable, some value-added features, assistance available through chat or phone.	Fee-based, requires a contract subscription, very reasonably priced. If your state bar association offers a subscription to either service as a benefit of membership, I highly encourage you to join that association.	Access from anywhere you have an internet or Wi-Fi connection and a laptop, smart phone, iPad, mobile device, etc.

Free Annotated or Unannotated State Statutes[51]		
GOOD	*CHEAP*	*FAST*
Good quality, updated, support	Great, if you happen to live in one of the	Access from anywhere you have

---

[51] LexisNexis® provides free public access to several of the annotated and unannotated codes they produce. A list of states is available at http://www.lexis nexis.com/hottopics/michie/ and include Arkansas, California, Colorado, Georgia,

available from the publisher, LexisNexis®.	twelve states where LexisNexis® provides an annotated or unannotated code available online to the public for free.[52]	an internet or Wi-Fi connection and a laptop, smart phone, iPad, mobile device, etc. CONS: Without annotations, and other value-added features, you may spend more time than using a fee or low-cost service.[53]

Federal Statutes http://uscode.house.gov/		
GOOD	**CHEAP**	*FAST*
The House of Representatives maintains the official source of codified federal statutes, prepared by the Office of the Law Revision Counsel of the	Zip, zero, nada dólares.[54] A great resource for the public. Not such a great resource for practicing attorneys.	Access from anywhere you have an internet or Wi-Fi connection and a laptop, smart phone, iPad, mobile device, etc.

Maryland, Massachusetts, Mississippi, New Jersey, Puerto Rico, Tennessee, Vermont, Virgin Islands, Washington, and Wyoming.

[52] Id.

[53] Why in the world would you, as a practicing attorney, rely on a resource for the public? Fastcase and Casemaker are low-cost, quality alternatives.

[54] Sadly, I am not bilingual, but I do know the value of a dollar, in any language.

United States House of Representatives.		CONS: Without annotations, and other value-added features, you may spend more time than using a fee or low-cost service.[55]
There are no annotations or other value-added features.		
There is no online or phone support.		

While you are researching statutes, look for any applicable statutes of limitations (or limitation of actions) that might limit or bar your client's ability to assert their claim. It is possible your client's injury occurred several years ago. Make sure the statutes you are researching were in effect at the time of your client's injury. If you are using Lexis Advance® or Westlaw Edge, it is easy to find prior versions of statutes. Look for the link to Archived Code Versions (on Lexis Advance®) or "Versions" under the History tab on Westlaw Edge. Finding superseded statutes on Fastcase and Casemaker is also easy. On Fastcase, choose the archived state statute and the version (2017 edition, 2016 edition, etc.).

Westlaw Edge has a new Compare Versions feature that makes it easier to compare how the language in an amended statute has recently changed.[56] If you are viewing a statute in Westlaw Edge, click on the Compare Versions button.[57] The language that has been recently added or changed will appear in light blue, while the

---

[55] Why in the world would you, as a practicing attorney, rely on a resource for the public? Fastcase and Casemaker are low-cost, quality alternatives.

[56] *Statutes Compare and Regulations Compare*, https://legal.thomsonreuters.com/en/products/westlaw/edge/statutes-compare-and-regulations-compare.

[57] This feature is not available on all statutory sections; only those statutory sections that have been recently revised or amended.

language that has been stricken or replaced will appear in red. The language that appears in black is currently in force and has not been amended or changed.

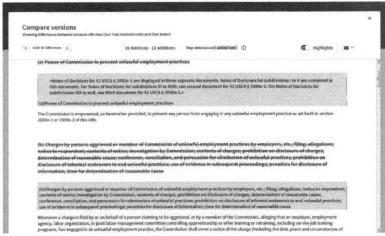

Reprinted from Westlaw with permission. Copyright 2019, Thomson Reuters. All rights reserved.

If the statutory language has changed, pay attention to the year the language was amended.[58] Any case law citing the statute will need to fall within the time range of the dates the statute was in effect. If your client's injury occurred after a statute was amended, say in 2009, do not use cases interpreting the law that was in effect prior to 2009. For example, the Act establishing the Commission on Equal Employment Opportunity was passed in 1964 and amended nearly fifty years later in 2009. This means nearly half a century of case law interpreted a law that is no longer in effect, but still appears linked to this statutory section. If your client filed their claim in 2010, the amended law was in effect and you should narrow your case law results to cases decided after 2009. The Case

---

[58] The history of a statute and any amendments will appear directly beneath the text of the section. On Lexis Advance®, go to the **History** of the statute. On Westlaw Edge, follow the **Currentness** link. On Fastcase, the statutory history will appear beneath the statutory text, along with any amendments to the section.

LITIGATION PHASE I: CASE ASSESSMENT PART 1:
IS THERE A VALID CAUSE OF ACTION?

59

Notes/Notes of Decision linked to each statutory section on Lexis Advance® and Westlaw Edge will also not change with amendments, so pay attention to your statute's history and make certain the case law you find is discussing the law that is currently in effect. This is another reason why it is not a good idea to begin your research in a case law database—you may inadvertently find case law that has been overruled by statute! While citation services like Shepard's and KeyCite will identify case law that has been overruled by statute, an amended statute will not trigger the same alerts.

2. Are You Prepared to Represent Your Client?

The three big legal research services (Bloomberg Law, Lexis Advance®, and Westlaw Edge) now provide content organized by select areas of law. The content of a Practical Guidance/Lexis Practice Advisor® page include all primary and secondary resources available from that legal research service under one general umbrella concept, such as employment law. The guidance pages are designed to assist lawyers by bringing all related content together in one place, instead of categorizing content by type or jurisdiction. If you are representing a client on an issue that is new to you, practical guidance pages are a good place to start. The guidance may help you determine whether your client's legal issue is one you will be comfortable handling.

a. Bloomberg Law Practical Guidance

Bloomberg Law offers hundreds of Practical Guidance pages. There is a **Litigation Intelligence Center**, and Practical Guidance pages that compile related resources for litigation and transactional practices. From the main menu, select **Practical Guidance** to view a list of subject specific resources. Bloomberg Law develops guidance pages as new areas of law evolve. Current subjects include: bankruptcy, commercial transactions, employment law, environmental, health care, litigation, and tax, among others. The Litigation resources provide guidance on Initiating Litigation, Injunctions & Temporary Restraining Orders, Responsive Pleadings & Motions, Threshold Issues & Defenses, and Default Judgments & Sanctions. The following screen shot shows a list of sample documents and guidance resources available for Initiating Litigation.[59]

For solo or small law firm attorneys, this type of guidance provides the expertise that is usually only available in large law firms with lawyers with years of specialization in one specific area.

---

[59]   Reprinted with permission by Bloomberg Law. Copyright 2019.

In addition, the Practical Guidance tools and features are *not* an additional cost; they are included in the annual subscription to Bloomberg Law.

b. *Lexis Advance® Suggested Questions & Lexis Practice Advisor®*

Lexis Advance® offers several options for finding related content on your issue. For example, type "employment discrimination" in the general search box of Lexis Advance® and you'll find a wealth of information on point with your client's legal issue. The suggested sources include leading treatises on employment discrimination you may not otherwise be familiar with if you did not take an employment law course in law school.

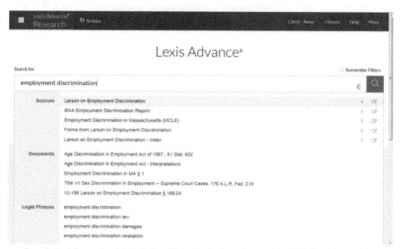

Reprinted from LexisNexis® with permission. Copyright 2019 LexisNexis®.
All rights reserved.

Entering a search for the broad issue of "employment discrimination" suggests several treatises and related laws to help us recognize we need to narrow our focus. Lexis Advance® also offers "Suggested Questions" to lead researchers to what they might actually need—*i.e.*, the elements of an employment discrimination claim, the legal definition, the leading case law, and/or what the burden of proof is—all excellent starting points requiring very little effort or time and no additional cost.

In addition to providing links to specific content, like an employment law treatise, Lexis Advance® also offers Lexis Practice Advisor® pages, where researchers can narrow by Practice Area, Content Type, Jurisdiction,[60] or Industry. To find the Lexis Practice Advisor® pages on Lexis Advance®, go to the matrix in the upper left-hand corner and select Lexis Practice Advisor®. Then search for your topic to find related content. Here is a list of practice areas available under Content Type, which includes a Labor & Employment practice area page.

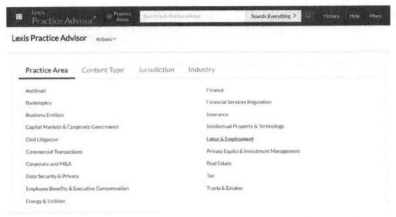

Reprinted from LexisNexis® with permission. Copyright 2019 LexisNexis®. All rights reserved.

The Labor & Employment practice area page provides links leading to resources that will help with the most common tasks. The idea is to streamline effort and reduce the amount of time lawyers spend

---

[60] Most of the content is aimed at supporting federal civil litigation. The Jurisdiction tab includes links to state content, but the content may be sparse.

researching an issue or tracking down boilerplate forms.[61] Additional content is available to assist with other common research needs, such as a State Law Comparison Tool and trending news on the subject.

Reprinted from LexisNexis® with permission. Copyright 2019 LexisNexis®. All rights reserved.

Alternatively, you can begin by selecting the Jurisdiction tab and then Practice Area:

---

[61] LEXISNEXIS, *Research and Practical Guidance That Work Hand in Hand*, https://www.lexisnexis.com/en-us/products/lexis-practice-advisor/lexis-advance-and-lexis-practice-advisor-integration.page.

Reprinted from LexisNexis® with permission. Copyright 2019 LexisNexis®.
All rights reserved.

Selecting the Labor & Employment practice area page will lead you to all related content available through Lexis Advance®. The default display is an alphabetical list of Practice Notes, although you can select other content on the left, such as Forms, Clauses, Checklists, etc.[62]

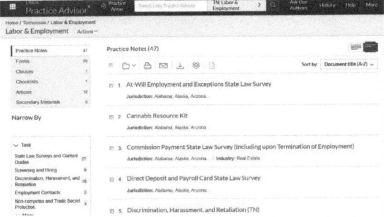

Reprinted from LexisNexis® with permission. Copyright 2019 LexisNexis®.
All rights reserved.

---

[62] LEXISNEXIS, *Document Types Available on Lexis Practice Advisor*, http://lexis nexis.custhelp.com/app/answers/answer_view/a_id/1087806/~/document-types-available-on-lexis-practice-advisor.

c. *Westlaw Edge Suggestions and Practical Law*

Westlaw Edge also provides auto fill and directed link, just by simply entering a search query. Entering "employment discrimination" into the general search box leads to Suggestions and related Content Pages. Researchers can also narrow the search results to display only cases, statutes, regulations, or secondary sources. Westlaw Edge provides case search Suggestions that lead to case law with related West Key Numbers on point with the research query.

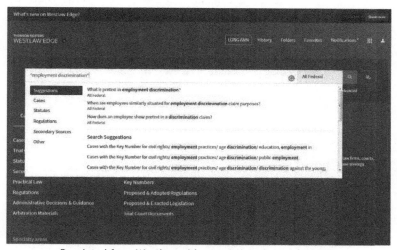

Reprinted from Westlaw with permission. Copyright 2019,
Thomson Reuters. All rights reserved.

Westlaw Edge has a new feature called Practical Law, "where legal know-how and legal research connect."[63] From the website,

---

[63] WESTLAW EDGE'S PRACTICAL LAW CONNECT, https://legal.thomsonreuters.com/en/products/practical-law/connect. "Our team of over 260 Practical Law attorney-editors create and maintain the Practice Notes, Checklists, Toolkits, Model Documents, and other how-to resources that give you a better starting place for any task. They also leverage their extensive practice experience at leading law firms, corporate legal departments, and government agencies to select the right resource for the job." Id.

Our team of over 260 Practical Law attorney-editors create and maintain the Practice Notes, Checklists, Toolkits, Model Documents, and other how-to resources that give you a better starting place for any task. They also leverage their extensive practice experience at leading law firms, corporate legal departments, and government agencies to select the right resource for the job.

If you are logged on to Westlaw Edge, select the drop down arrow (on the left) and select Practical Law to change your view. Then you can select from a list of Practice Areas, Resource Types, or Jurisdictions to begin your research.

Reprinted from Westlaw with permission. Copyright 2019,
Thomson Reuters. All rights reserved.

The Labor & Employment practice area page display defaults to additional subtopics to help streamline your research.

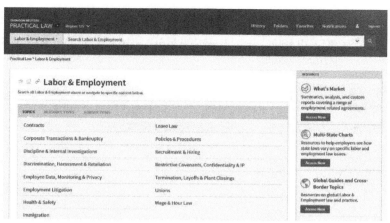

Reprinted from Westlaw with permission. Copyright 2019,
Thomson Reuters. All rights reserved.

Selecting the subtopic of Discrimination, Harassment & Retaliation leads to an alphabetical display of Westlaw's Practice Notes.[64]

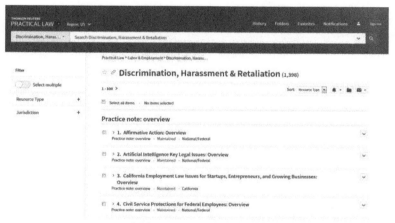

Reprinted from Westlaw with permission. Copyright 2019,
Thomson Reuters. All rights reserved.

---

[64] WESTLAW, *Discover Practical Law: A Legal Know-How to a Better Start*, https://lawschool.westlaw.com/marketing/display/PL/1.

While the majority of the information is related to federal litigation, researchers can select the Litigation State Q&A and narrow by topic or jurisdiction:

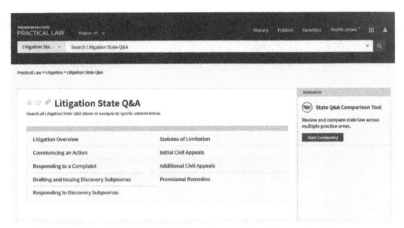

Reprinted from Westlaw with permission. Copyright 2019, Thomson Reuters. All rights reserved.

Reprinted from Westlaw with permission. Copyright 2019, Thomson Reuters. All rights reserved.

Considering all of the information provided from a legal research service,[65] why would you begin your legal research query with Google?

---

[65] Searching on Lexis Advance® and Westlaw Edge is free, or at no additional charge, if you have a subscription to either service. Lexis Advance® and Westlaw Edge

Practical Guidance		
GOOD	~~**CHEAP**~~[66]	**FAST!** *timesaver!*
Bloomberg Law Practical Guidance and Litigation Intelligence Center[67] **Lexis Practice Advisor®** **Westlaw Edge Practical Guidance**	Bloomberg Law's annual subscription price includes *everything*, including all intelligence center content. The practical guidance/advisor content available through Lexis Advance® and Westlaw Edge are an add-on to your existing contract. Contact your representative for more information and a free trial.	All of the practical guidance pages are timesavers! Provides expertise without the learning curve. Best for federal civil litigation. Check each service for specific content. All research services offer a free trial period.

Answers are also free. If you have a subscription to Westlaw Edge and use transactional billing, "the monthly fee covers searching for documents, viewing documents from content included in your plan, and offline delivery of documents (printing or downloading)." Westlaw Pricing Guidelines, *supra*, note 44. Lexis Advance® does not provide pricing guidelines to academics. All of the content available on Bloomberg Law is available for one price—there is not an option to opt in or out of content.

[66] Although the pricing of these resources may seem high, consider what you are paying for: advice. If you are a solo, or in a small law firm, it may be worth the investment. If you bill your time at $100/hour, you would pay for this content in less than a day. It's not always easy to get mentoring or advice when you need it at the exact time you need it, and online content is available 24/7!

[67] Robert Ambrogi, *Bloomberg Law Expands its Litigation Coverage with New Practical Guidance Content*, LawSites (May 21, 2019), https://www.lawsitesblog.com/2019/05/bloomberg-law-expands-its-litigation-coverage-with-new-practical-guidance-content.html.

CHAPTER 3

Litigation Phase I: Case Assessment Part 2: Is the Issue Worth Pursuing?

Now that you have researched the law and decided your client has a valid cause of action, you need to decide if it is an action worth pursuing. There are several things to consider when you agree to represent your client—the amount of time, cost, and scope of representation are all reasonable considerations for new or solo lawyers.

1. How Much Time Will It Take?

While there might not be any way to determine the exact amount of time you will spend on a civil litigation matter, you can research the court system's docket schedule, court rules, and verdicts to gain a greater understanding of what you can expect. The Administrative Office of the United States Courts is required to "provide a report of statistical information on the caseload of the federal courts for the 12-month period ending March 31" and provide "data on the work of the appellate, district, and bankruptcy courts and the probation and pretrial services systems."[1] State court caseload statistics are available through an interactive tool provided by the Court Statistics Project.[2]

FindLaw has an article on Lawsuit Chronology that attempts to explain the process of civil litigation to non-lawyers, which may be helpful if you need to explain the process to your client.[3] In law, everything is based on precedent. This is also true for finding practical advice. There may be a lawyer who is an expert in your practice area or jurisdiction, and may have written an article or treatise on the subject. Recently, all the major legal research services have developed litigation platforms to assist with the practice of civil litigation. Although the federal resources far outweigh the state resources, many of these resources also provide general guidance for all types of civil litigation.

a.　*Time from Initial Filing to Final Disposition*

Trying to figure out how many weeks or months the litigation process will take is now a little easier to do, thanks to artificial intelligence and the recent explosion of litigation analytics. Legal AI is based on existing case law and related court docket data, but a computer can compile and analyze this information much faster than a human.[4] All of the major legal research services offer some type of litigation analytics and much of that data stems from the

---

[1]　UNITED STATES COURTS, *Federal Judicial Caseload Statistics 2018*, https://www.uscourts.gov/statistics-reports/federal-judicial-caseload-statistics-2018.

[2]　Go to the Court Statistics Project's website at http://www.courtstatistics.org/ and select the type of case (criminal or civil), state, and court.

[3]　*What to Expect: A Lawsuit Chronology*, FINDLAW, https://litigation.findlaw.com/filing-a-lawsuit/what-to-expect-a-lawsuit-chronology.html.

[4]　Liqun Luo, *Why is the Human Brain so Efficient? How Massive Parallelism Lifts the Brain's Performance Above That of AI*, NAUTILUS (Apr. 12, 2018), http://nautil.us/issue/59/connections/why-is-the-human-brain-so-efficient (explaining that while the human brain is 10 million times slower than a computer, the human brain "employs massive parallel processing" which allows humans to make connections that computers can't).

LITIGATION PHASE I: CASE ASSESSMENT PART 2:
IS THE ISSUE WORTH PURSUING?

73

same source: publicly available electronic federal and state dockets.

Having access to litigation analytics will help lawyers give better advice to their clients on the amount of time and potential outcome they can expect in any particular court. Prior to litigation analytics, attorneys were limited to what they could learn from decisions in case law databases or information reported in jury verdict and settlement reporters. The number of cases that make it all the way to a written opinion are comparatively rare to the actual number of cases filed. The U.S. Courts website provides data on the number of cases filed by court and date.[5] In 2018, the U.S. Federal District Courts received a total of 225,328 cases filed, but only a mere fraction of those cases—2,196—were resolved by a trial.[6] Prior to the litigation analytics databases, the only information lawyers could provide to their clients was the likely amount of time it would take for their case to be heard/resolved in the court they filed in, based on the prior year's data.[7]

---

[5] U.S. COURTS, *Federal Judicial Caseload Statistics*, https://www.uscourts.gov/statistics-reports.

[6] Id.

[7] Visit the U.S. Court's website to find out how quickly courts handle cases from the Federal Judicial Caseload Statistics, Id.; or the Court Statistics Project's website for state caseload statistics, COURT STATISTICS PROJECT, *Civil Caseloads (2016)*, http://www.courtstatistics.org/NCSC-Analysis/Civil.aspx.

Table C-5. U.S. District Courts—Median Time Intervals From Filing to Disposition of Civil Cases Terminated, by District and Method of Disposition, During the 12-Month Period Ending March 31, 2018										
	Total Cases		No Court Action		Court Action					
					Before Pretrial		During or After Pretrial		During Trial	
Circuit and District	Number of Cases	Median Time Interval in Months	Number of Cases	Median Time Interval in Months	Number of Cases	Median Time Interval in Months	Number of Cases	Median Time Interval in Months	Number of Cases	Median Time Interval in Months
Total	225,328	10.1	41,425	4.8	152,986	11.2	28,721	12.6	2,196	25.4
DC	2,207	6.6	972	4.4	1,205	8.9	10	35.4	20	44.6
1st	6,284	13.3	1,694	8.7	3,003	12.4	1,501	19.4	86	31.9
ME	467	8.2	165	6.7	275	9.3	15	14.4	12	18.8
MA	3,553	17.6	935	7.9	1,317	18.2	1,245	19.7	56	33.1
NH	382	9.7	68	3.7	212	8.7	98	17.1	4	.
RI	535	9.6	35	13.1	418	8.5	79	14.8	3	.
PR	1,347	13.7	491	11.7	781	14.1	64	25.5	11	38.6
2nd	20,823	8.1	3,346	3.6	11,888	7.3	5,311	13.8	278	34.3
CT	1,852	10.2	316	3.7	946	8.9	554	15.6	37	34.1
NY,N	1,112	10.2	131	3.1	638	10.3	315	14.6	28	39.0

While this information is helpful for venue shopping and finding "rocket dockets," any information on how a judge would rule on an issue was limited to case law decisions or clerk insights.[8] Now, all the data points available in a court cover sheet, and all public court filings are now fodder for analysis.

Additionally, if you are a plaintiff's lawyer, and if you agree to take a case on a contingency basis, it is imperative that the lawyer does not spend a lot of unexpected time or money in legal research fees.

> In a contingent fee arrangement, the lawyer agrees to accept a fixed percentage (often one third) of the recovery, which is the amount finally paid to the client. If you win the case, the lawyer's fee comes out of the money awarded to you. If you lose, neither you nor the

---

[8]   However, the ALMANAC OF THE FEDERAL JUDICIARY (published by Thomson Reuters and available on Westlaw) provides anonymous comments from former court clerks on the judges they worked with. These insights are used to determine how a judge may lean on issues that may not be apparent in written decisions, such as whether the judge would consider legislative histories or only black letter law.

lawyer will get any money, but you will not be required
to pay your attorney for the work done on the case.[9]

Doing a bit of research on the amount of time cases similar to your
case take to work their way through a court's docket system
(researching either the cause of action or nature of suit) will help
gauge how much time you expect the representation to last and
whether you believe your efforts will be successful.

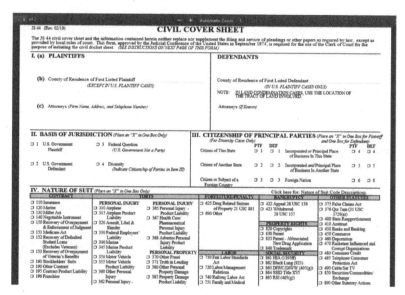

The data has been available through PACER and other court filing
systems, such as CourtLink, for decades. For example, if you wanted
to find all cases filed with a certain Nature of Suit (NOS) against a
defendant, you could easily search for and find that information.
Additionally, if you wanted to find all of the cases a particular judge
has reviewed for a certain NOS or COA, you could easily find that
information. However, sorting through all of those filings to build a
consensus on how a judge would likely rule on future cases involving

---

9   AMERICAN BAR ASSOCIATION, *Legal Fees and Expenses: What Are Contingent Fees?*
(Mar.18, 2013), https://www.americanbar.org/groups/public_education/resources/
law_issues_for_consumers/lawyerfees_contingent/.

similar issues required a great deal of manpower hours. In the past, this type of analysis was limited to large law firms with available human resources, usually requiring law librarians and paralegals to work together to find and analyze the data. The new litigation analytics features help level the litigation playing field by allowing solo and small law firms access to the same information, for a price.

The utility of AI for the practice of law has been discussed in legal circles for decades.[10] Legal arguments are based on past precedent and the entire legal system is organized hierarchically. Legal scholars have been considering the potential for future applications of legal data long before most attorneys were using computers or submitting their documents through electronic case management systems.[11] For our current purposes, if you are interested in learning how quickly a case moves from initiation to resolution, begin by finding out whether your court has an electronic case management filing system (refer to either the PACER website for federal courts, or the National Center for State Courts list of state courts).[12] Next, you can visit the U.S. Court's website to find out how quickly courts handle cases from the Federal Judicial Caseload Statistics or the Court Statistics Project's website for state caseload statistics.[13] However, now litigation analytics offer options for compiling and analyzing the data you need, in additional to the potential time investment, depending on the research service.

---

[10]   Bruce G. Buchanan & Thomas E. Headrick, *Some Speculation about Artificial Intelligence and Legal Reasoning*, 23 STAN. L. REV. 40 (1970).

[11]   Id.

[12]   COURT STATISTICS PROJECT, *Civil Caseloads (2016)*, http://www.courtstatistics. org/NCSC-Analysis/Civil.aspx. Also check with your state court's website for more current and complete information.

[13]   U.S. COURTS, *Federal Judicial Caseload Statistics*, https://www.uscourts.gov/ statistics-reports.

b. Fastcase's Docket Alarm and Analytics Workbench

Let's begin with the most affordable option. If you have access to Fastcase, consider adding Docket Alarm to your bar membership subscription. At only $99/month,[14] it will provide you with an inexpensive option for searching state and federal dockets. Unfortunately, if you are only looking for the time it will take any particular court or judge to decide on an issue, you will also need to subscribe to the Analytics Workbench.

> . . .users can build litigation analytics across all case types in state courts, federal courts, administrative courts, and other jurisdictions in the Docket Alarm system. In addition to expanded analytics court coverage, the Analytics Workbench allows legal professionals to dig deeper. Users can capture and analyze legal events that remain hidden in traditional offerings. For example, the Analytics Workbench can uncover trends about discovery motions, *motions in limine*, and scheduling and pre-trial conferences, at both the state and federal level that would be impossible for traditional analytics.[15]

There is a wealth of information available in state and federal dockets and the Analytics Workbench provides the tools to customize the data for each new client and legal issue. The graphics are by far the most beautiful of any analytics provider and the ability to customize the data is unique. Here is an example of the specific type of data sets you can create—the graph below shows

---

[14]   Not including PACER fees. Monthly pricing from 2019 and is subject to change.

[15]   FASTCASE, *Docket Alarm's "Analytics Workbench" Pioneers Customizable Legal Analytics for All Cases, All Practice Areas,* https://www.fastcase.com/blog/docket-alarms-analytics-workbench-pioneers-customizable-legal-analytics-for-all-cases-all-practice-areas/.

the number of preliminary injunctions granted or denied in New York federal courts for civil cases:[16]

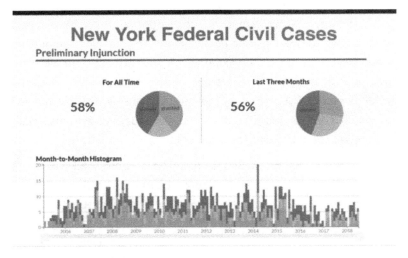

c. *Lexis Advance® Litigation Profile Suite & Lex Machina®*

In the initial stages of litigation, it is unlikely you will know which judge will be assigned to your case, but you will know the court. If you know the court, you can research all of the judges. Using the Litigation Profile Suite in Lexis Advance®, let's search for the Hon. Aleta Trauger from the U.S. District Court in the Middle District of Tennessee.

---

[16] Id.

LITIGATION PHASE I: CASE ASSESSMENT PART 2:
IS THE ISSUE WORTH PURSUING?

79

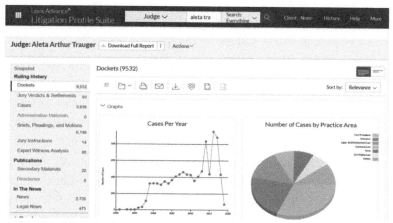

Reprinted from LexisNexis® with permission. Copyright 2019 LexisNexis®.
All rights reserved.

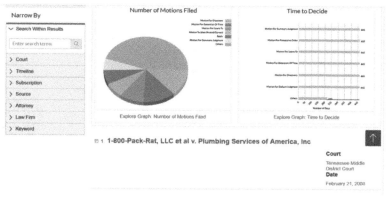

Reprinted from LexisNexis® with permission. Copyright 2019 LexisNexis®.
All rights reserved.

Looking at the information from the *Number of Cases by Practice Area*, it will come as no surprise that the most common motion is a Motion for Summary Judgment, because Civil Procedure is the subject area with the highest number of cases filed. Expanding the *Time to Decide* chart shows, interestingly, that it will take 465 days for Judge Trauger to decide any type of motion. With this information, you can advise your client that it will likely take more than a year (15.2 months) to pursue litigation in the Middle District of Tennessee in Judge Trauger's court.

If you are forum shopping and trying to decide whether to file in the Middle District or Eastern District of Tennessee, using Lexis Advance®, you would need to research all of the judges in each court. However, if you begin your research in a case law database, narrow your jurisdiction to the **Federal District Courts in Tennessee** and search for a specific case type, such as employment, you can link to the Litigation Analytics from Lex Machina®.[17] Look on the right hand side and expand the Legal Analytics option to link to the Lex Machina® data.

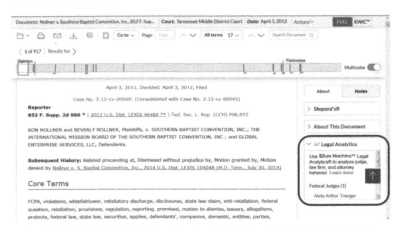

Reprinted from LexisNexis® with permission. Copyright 2019 LexisNexis®. All rights reserved.

The Lex Machina profile includes Judge Trauger's Open Cases side-by-side to other open cases in the Middle District of Tennessee. For Employment cases, Judge Trauger appears to handle 35.5% of cases.

---

17   Not available for all judges.

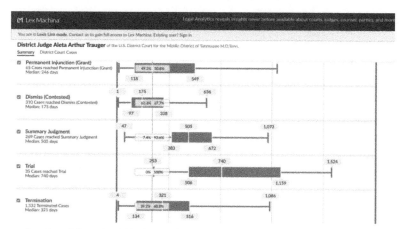

Reprinted from LexisNexis® with permission. Copyright 2019 LexisNexis®.
All rights reserved.

Scrolling down to view a Summary of Motion Types and Time to Resolution, it appears that only 35 cases on Judge Trauger's docket ever make it to trial, and if they do, it will take 740 days (or more than two years). Even case dismissals take an average of 97 days, or about three months.

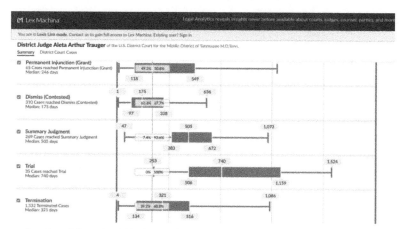

Reprinted from LexisNexis® with permission. Copyright 2019 LexisNexis®.
All rights reserved.

Not all judges have Lex Machina profiles[18] that provide additional information about the judge and comparisons to other judges within the court where they sit. Lex Machina currently evaluates fifteen litigation practice areas, which include antitrust, bankruptcy, contract, copyright, Delaware Chancery Court, employment, environmental, ERISA, insurance, patent, product liability, securities, tax, trademark, and trade secret litigation.[19] If your judge has been involved in any one of these fifteen types of cases, you will be able to find a limited profile on that judge's decisions and past behavior.

d. *Westlaw Edge Litigation Analytics*

Westlaw Edge has the only litigation analytics searchable by Court. All other research services offer search options by individual judge. To access the litigation analytics on Westlaw Edge, begin by selecting *Litigation Analytics* and then search by Judge, Court, Attorney, Law Firm, or Case Type. This example provides an Overview of the Northern District of Georgia.

---

[18]   Lex Machina® offers select areas of law, which means only judges that have decided cases in those areas will have profiles. LEXISNEXIS, *Lex Machina: Practice Areas*, https://lexmachina.com/practice-areas/.

[19]   Id.

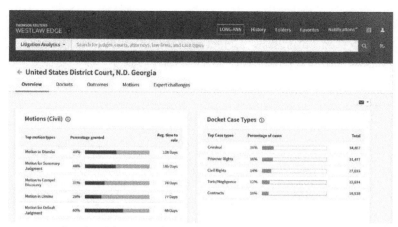

Reprinted from Westlaw with permission. Copyright 2019,
Thomson Reuters. All rights reserved.

In the Northern District of Georgia, nearly half of all Motions to Dismiss and Motions for Summary Judgment occur in fewer than 185 days (or less than six months).

For more detailed information on a specific type of case, select the Outcomes view.

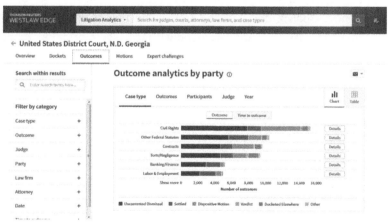

Reprinted from Westlaw with permission. Copyright 2019,
Thomson Reuters. All rights reserved.

In the above example, the majority of all case types resulted in an uncontested dismissal. Selecting the Details for Labor & Employment practice area page shows that 38% of cases settled and 44% resulted in an uncontested dismissal.

Labor & Employment			☒
Outcome		**Percentage**	**Total**
Uncontested Dismissal		44%	2,213
Settled		38%	1,899
Dispositive Motion		13%	672
Verdict		<1%	41
Docketed Elsewhere		3%	139
Other		2%	76

Reprinted from Westlaw with permission. Copyright 2019, Thomson Reuters. All rights reserved.

The Litigation Analytics are also integrated in the case law databases on Westlaw Edge. If you begin research in a Georgia case law database (either state or federal) and search for the phrase "employment discrimination" the Westlaw results can be sorted by relevance, date, most cited, most used, court level, and term frequency. Open a decision and follow the link to the judge who decided the case to learn more about that judge's prior decisions for similar case types.

LITIGATION PHASE I: CASE ASSESSMENT PART 2:
IS THE ISSUE WORTH PURSUING?

85

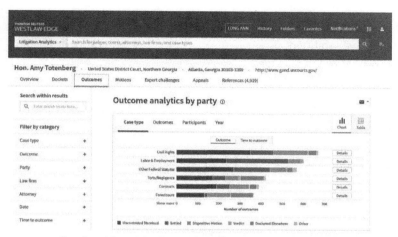

Reprinted from Westlaw with permission. Copyright 2019,
Thomson Reuters. All rights reserved.

In the above example. Hon. Amy Totenberg appears to settle more labor and employment cases than almost any other type of case on her docket.

Litigation Analytics		
GOOD	*CHEAP*	FAST!
Fastcase Docket Alarm and Analytics Workbench Best for patent and trademark cases, also good for state and county dockets. Includes federal magistrate and bankruptcy dockets. Currently only 15 states are available	Fastcase's Docket Alarm is $99/month per individual user and does not include PACER fees. Contact Fastcase for pricing on the Analytics Workbench.	Timesaver! The Analytics Workbench is completely customizable. The Patent Trial and Appeal Board (PTAB) Predictive Analytics "can help predict outcomes in *inter partes* reviews or

(based mostly on the availability of state ECMs).		covered business method reviews."[21]
Lexis Advance® Litigation Suite and Lex Machina® Search by judge or expert witness. Regulatory and transactional tracking are also available.[20]	The litigation analytics available through Lexis Advance® and Westlaw Edge are an add-on to your existing contract.	LexisNexis® claims that their legal analytics has "the most accurate and comprehensive information to inform your decisions and build your argument."[22]
Westlaw Edge Litigation Analytics Only service that offers searching by court (not just by individual judge). Federal magistrate and bankruptcy dockets are not included.	Contact your local representative for more information on pricing and a free trial.	Westlaw claims to have the most data from federal and state courts than any other service.[23]

[20] Bob Ambrogi, *LexisNexis Launches Lexis Analytics, Putting a "Stake in the Ground" to Claim the Legal Analytics Space*, LawSites (July 13, 2018), https://www.lawsitesblog.com/2018/07/lexisnexis-launches-lexis-analytics-putting-stake-ground-claim-legal-analytics-space.html.

[21] Docket Alarm, *PTAB Predictive Analytics*, https://www.docketalarm.com/features#analytics-histogram.

[22] LexisNexis, *A Buyer's Guide to Choosing the Right Legal Analytics*, https://www.lexisnexis.com/pdf/context/lexisnexis-legal-analytics-buyers-guide.pdf.

[23] Bob Ambrogi, *Move Over Westlaw—Meet the Next-Generation Westlaw Edge, With Advanced AI and Analytics*, LawSites (July 12, 2018), https://www.lawsitesblog.com/2018/07/move-westlaw-meet-next-generation-westlaw-edge-advanced-ai-analytics.html.

LITIGATION PHASE I: CASE ASSESSMENT PART 2:
IS THE ISSUE WORTH PURSUING?

87

2. What's It Worth? Jury Verdicts and Settlements

By now, you have established your client has a valid cause of action and understand the approximate amount of time it will take to resolve. The last piece of the puzzle is to figure out what your client can expect to receive in monetary damages. *Jury Verdicts & Settlements* databases are an excellent place to begin. There are verdicts and settlements databases by jurisdiction and practice area on all research services. The jury verdict and settlement data may be your only insight into state trial court judge's behavior. Additionally, some law firms post their successful verdicts and settlements on their web pages, if you are looking for specific city or county data.

a. *Lawyers Weekly Newsletters*

Lawyers Weekly publishes newsletters in several states to cover state trial court information.[24] There is a section that highlights verdicts and settlements reported by lawyers who submit their own trial successes. From the *Virginia Lawyers Weekly* website:

> Welcome to Virginia Lawyers Weekly's new Verdicts & Settlements research database. This beta version will be available for free to subscribers for a limited time. This powerful online tool allows you to search verdict and settlements throughout the state. The VLW V&S database will help you compare your own cases and assess their value for trial or settlement. You also can learn more about a particular city or county, court, judge, expert or opposing counsel. Anyone may submit a new verdict or settlement for publication in Virginia Lawyers Weekly.

---

[24] *Lawyers Weekly* publishes newsletters for Massachusetts, Michigan, Missouri, North Carolina, South Carolina, and Virginia.

Once published, the details also will be entered into the V&S database, but only Virginia Lawyers Weekly subscribers are able to view and search the entire system.[25]

The *Lawyers Weekly* newsletters are also available on Lexis Advance®. On Lexis Advance®, you can create an alert for a particular case type or judge's name, to track case outcomes in your jurisdiction.

b. *VerdictSearch*

Another resource, *VerdictSearch*, is another publication that encourages attorneys to submit the results of civil litigation at the trial court level. From the VerdictSearch website:

You can use the form below or call 212-457-9576 to report a recent civil verdict or settlement to VerdictSearch. Reporting cases to VerdictSearch is a great way to get published: All verdicts and settlements reported are eligible for publication in VerdictSearch newsletters and other ALM publications including: *National Law Journal, New York Law Journal, Texas Lawyer, Legal Times* and *The Recorder*.[26]

To search the outcomes in the VerdictSearch database, consider using Google as your search engine. Google can search a specific website for your keywords by using the following formula:

---

[25] VIRGINIA LAWYERS WEEKLY, http://verdicts.valawyersweekly.com/.

[26] VERDICTSEARCH, a product of ALM intelligence, https://verdictsearch.com/ submit-case/.

Example: site:verdictsearch.com and gender discrimination

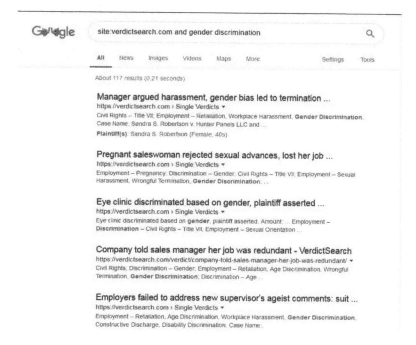

As you can see from the above screenshot, the only results Google returns are from the VerdictSearch website and they all deal with gender discrimination. This search strategy will also work on other websites. VerdictSearch newsletters and ALM publications are also available on Lexis Advance®.

c. *Lexis Advance® Jury Verdicts and Settlements*

On Lexis Advance®, select *Jury Verdicts and Settlements* from the Content Type tab. Then narrow by federal circuit, state, or practice area. Again, AI provides us with a lot of interesting content. There have been jury verdict and settlement resources for years, but the addition of AI allows us to sort this data in more meaningful ways, and much faster. Selecting the Labor & Employment Law practice area, Discrimination, and narrowing to the Sixth Circuit returns nearly 600 results. Following the link to the *Lexis Advance®* *Verdicts & Settlements Analyzer*, we can see the data displayed in various graphical formats.

Reprinted from LexisNexis® with permission. Copyright 2019 LexisNexis®. All rights reserved.

Looking at the first graph, *Number of Cases Per Year by Resolution*, we can see that in the past five years, most cases have settled. However, beginning in 2018, most cases were resolved through arbitration, in favor of the defendant. The third graph, *Awards in U.S. Dollars by Resolution*, shows that the average award for a plaintiff's verdict is over 1.6 million! The *Percentage of Cases by Resolution* shows that 34% of the cases are resolved in favor of plaintiffs, which is only slightly higher than the 29% of the cases

LITIGATION PHASE I: CASE ASSESSMENT PART 2:
IS THE ISSUE WORTH PURSUING?

91

resolved in favor of defendants, and the 26% of the cases that were settled. For more specific information, sort the data on the left (by Court, Case Resolution, Timeline, Award Amount, or Injury) and read the following case summaries. The case summaries are displayed beneath the graphs and can be sorted by Relevance, or by any of the fields on the left.

d. *Westlaw Edge Jury Verdicts and Settlements*

On Westlaw Edge, begin by selecting *Jury Verdicts & Settlements* from the Content Type tab. Then narrow by state, federal circuit, or practice area before entering your search terms. Selecting the Labor & Employment Jury Verdicts & Settlements and searching for **retaliation and discrimination**, results in more than 2,000 case summaries. Narrowing the result to the federal district courts in the Sixth Circuit (on the left) returns almost 170 case summaries. Unlike Lexis Advance® and Bloomberg Law, Westlaw Edge does not appear to incorporate any litigation analytics with their jury verdicts and settlements case summaries.

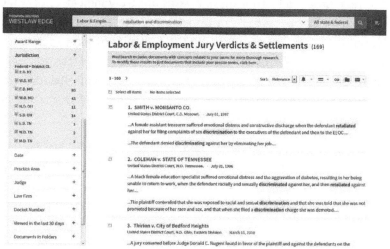

Reprinted from Westlaw with permission. Copyright 2019,
Thomson Reuters. All rights reserved.

e. *Bloomberg Law Trackers*

Bloomberg Law does not offer any jury verdict information, but does offer a broad array of legislative and regulatory "trackers." From the main menu of Bloomberg Law, select Browse, Practitioner Tools, then Trackers. The trackers are organized by subject and monitor changes and developments in state legislation regulations. Current trackers include: Banking & Finance, Benefits & Executive Compensation, Corporate & Securities, General Litigation, Health Care, Intellectual Property, Labor & Employment, Privacy & Data Security, and Tax. It is important to monitor legislative and regulatory changes of interest to your clients. Staying abreast of changes in the law may help keep your client out of court!

If you are heading to court, using the trackers and jury verdict resources above will help you advise your client on the likely outcome. Although the results from any of the jury verdict and settlement databases shown above look promising, you should access the docket and read each of the associated complaints and the final order to learn if these awards are truly indicative of what your client can expect. Read through the related documents from the cases that have been successful to find out how best to prepare your case. Also, research the law firms and the attorneys who represented successful clients. There are litigation analytics for attorneys and law firms, which might be a good first step in researching opposing counsel.

Regardless of the resource you begin with, please understand the majority of self-reported verdicts are favorable to the attorney or law firm providing the information. There are jury verdict and settlement case summaries that include a $0 award, but most likely, the data will be skewed more favorably toward successful litigants with significantly large awards. However, with the addition of artificial intelligence, the jury verdict and settlement data can be analyzed with other court data to provide a more complete picture.

Jury Verdicts & Settlements		
GOOD	**CHEAP**	**FAST!**
Lawyers Weekly newsletters

VerdictSearch

Lexis Advance® Jury Verdicts & Settlements

Westlaw Edge Jury Verdicts & Settlements | A *Virginia Lawyers Weekly* subscription is $19 for the first month, then $39/month thereafter.[27]

VerdictSearch is $395 for a day pass or $99/month for solo practitioners.[28]

May be an add-on to your existing Lexis Advance® or Westlaw subscription.

The Westlaw Jury Verdicts and Settlements databases are available through the Westlaw Patron subscription, available through court and select | For state trial courts, jury verdict and settlement information may be your only source for predicting a likely outcome (state trial courts do not publish their decisions). Fastest way to determine a likely award amount for similar case types in your jurisdiction. |

---

[27] VIRGINIA LAWYERS WEEKLY, https://valawyersweekly.com/subscribe/.
[28] LAW.COM VERDICTSEARCH, https://verdictsearch.com/plans-pricing/.

	academic law libraries.	
Bloomberg Law Trackers	All content available on Bloomberg Law is available for the annual subscription price.	

3. Be Careful! Inaccuracies Abound!

Although litigation analytics are visually impressive and a potential time saver, please understand the data may be flawed. There is a law librarians' listserv[29] where law librarians across the country discuss everything related to legal research. With the recent explosion of litigation analytics, an "error of the day" post has begun. Law librarians from academic, court, and law firm libraries are finding inaccuracies in the data made available through the analytics on Lexis Advance®, Westlaw Edge, and other legal research services. Once an error has been identified and shared with the listserv, the responsible research service will respond with how the error has likely occurred and an explanation of how the research service's engineers are working to resolve the error. It's a little alarming that new errors are found every day!

Some of these errors are bad links or typos, but some of the errors could taint the results of litigation analytics derived from the search algorithms or artificial intelligence.[30] As the saying goes, bad

---

[29] Lawlib is the law librarian's listserv hosted by U.C. Davis. Mary E. Matuszak, Director of Library Services at the New York County District Attorney's Office, posts most of the errors. Ms. Matuszak compiled a spreadsheet of errors she had tracked since mid-October-December 2018 and there were more than 40 errors! Spreadsheet on file with author. In 2019, an error has been reported to the listserv almost every day!

[30] Legal vendor representatives also subscribe to the law librarians' listserv and alert the powers-that-be within their organization of the inaccuracies. The vendor

LITIGATION PHASE I: CASE ASSESSMENT PART 2:
IS THE ISSUE WORTH PURSUING?

95

data in, bad data out.[31] Some of the errors reported on the listserv include inaccurate dates, data linked to different judges or lawyers with the same or a similar name, or jurisdictions confused with similar abbreviations (is VA for Virginia or Veteran's Affairs?). Often the inaccuracies stem directly from the source inputting the information, such as court personnel or pro se patrons. Humans and computers alike make mistakes. Use the information gleaned from AI as one additional resource *but not the only resource* to help you advise your client on reasonable expectations for litigation.

There does not appear to be a "one size fits all" service, which should surprise no one who has ever tried to compare the legal research content of two or more research services. The twenty-seven law librarians who evaluated the litigation analytics of seven research services with sixteen "real world questions" found that "these platforms do slightly different things and work in slightly different ways so there is no real winner. And the platforms work best when they are run by experienced, well trained people who then manually review and analyze the results."[32] If you find yourself getting frustrated, you are not alone. Stay tuned and remain diligent! Research services that offer legal analytics and AI are continuing to develop and improve their platforms.[33] If you are interested in staying on top of all the developments of the 50+ research platforms, you may want to subscribe to the Legal AI Efficacy Report for a mere $4,995.[34]

---

representatives will respond to the error post with an acknowledgement of the problem and when the error will be fixed. If you find errors in your research data, contact the publisher and report it.

[31] Eric Shrok, *Regulations Won't Kill AI—Bad Data Will*, FORBES (Sept. 4, 2018), https://www.forbes.com/sites/forbestechcouncil/2018/09/04/regulations-wont-kill-ai-bad-data-will/#57bcb2e63405.

[32] Stephen Embry, *AALL's Litigation Data Analytics Competition: 5 Take Aways*, TECHLAW CROSSROADS (Jul. 15, 2019), https://www.techlawcrossroads.com/2019/07/aalls-litigation-data-analytics-competition-5-take-aways/.

[33] Id.

[34] *Blickstein Group Legal AI Efficacy Report*, https://newlaw.blicksteingroup.com/legal-ai-efficacy-report.

CHAPTER 4

Litigation Phase II: Discovery and Investigation

During the discovery and investigation phase, the goal is to find out everything else you need to know to prepare for litigation. During this phase, you will learn all the facts about your client's case and "discover" the facts about the opposing counsel's case. The goal of discovery is for all parties to learn what the other side knows, in order to remove any potential surprises at trial. The other goal is to determine the holes in your opponent's case. Often, the decision to move forward with litigation will become clear during this phase and may be dependent on the amount of money your client is willing to spend. If you are new to litigation, there are many resources that can help guide you through this stage and save you time and money.

1. Depositions, Interrogatories, and Checklists

Before you can begin deposing witnesses, you need to understand the related court rules and what information you are trying to find to support your client's case. Once again, we turn to secondary sources to explain and guide us through this process, and ultimately, save time. One good resource found in any academic law library, some court libraries, and on Westlaw Edge is AMERICAN JURISPRUDENCE TRIALS (AM. JUR. TRIALS).[1] The articles can be broad or very narrow in scope and help explain the process of deposing a witness and suggestions on how to ask questions that will give you the information you need. Additionally, you will need to prepare your own witnesses for deposition by opposing counsel. In this case, the article, "Surviving and Thriving in the Process of Preparing a Witness for Deposition"[2] might be a good article to read. If you can find an article related to your client's issue, you can find a wealth of advice from an attorney who has already navigated those waters. Each article includes an Article Outline, an Index, and additional Research Resources linked to the article that will provide further information.

AM. JUR. TRIALS articles begin with an introduction, or the scope of the article's coverage. Similar to a CAUSES OF ACTION article, the AM. JUR. TRIALS articles then discuss the legal background, and provide sample pleadings, the goals of discovery, sample pretrial motions, and trial suggestions (sample opening statements, direct and cross-examination, closing arguments, and related jury instructions). Finding an AM. JUR. TRIALS article on your client's issue will help prepare you for what you can expect during litigation and help you assess whether the case will settle, or go to trial.

---

[1]   "*American Jurisprudence Trials* contains articles authored by practicing attorneys and covers all areas of litigation. The articles provide trial-tested litigation tools to secure better settlements and verdicts. . . The authors detail successful strategies, and caution about unsuccessful ones, for every stage of trial—from initial client interview, pretrial motions, jury selection, and trial itself, to post-trial motions—to give practitioners the perspectives and tools necessary to succeed. In *American Jurisprudence Trials*, you'll find practical tips on admitting and preventing the admission of evidence, navigating complex procedural law, distinguishing unfavorable facts, and much more." Westlaw Scope Information.

[2]   Katherine James, *Surviving and Thriving in the Process of Preparing a Witness for Deposition*, 87 AM. JUR. TRIALS 1 (originally published in 2003; May 2018 update). Please see the article's outline, from Westlaw Edge, on the next page.

Surviving and Thriving in the Process of Preparing a Witness for Deposition

TABLE OF CONTENTS

Article Outline

Index

Research References

ARTICLE OUTLINE

I Introduction

§ 1 In general

§ 2 Overview

§ 2.1 Overview—Deponent privileges

§ 2.5 Overview—Apex deposition strategies

II Learning, Listening, and Processing

§ 3 In general

§ 4 Learning styles

§ 5 "Learner type"

§ 6 Witness "learner type"

§ 7 Listening mode

§ 8 Witness listening mode

§ 9 Processing type; visual, auditory or kinesthetic

III Rehearsal

§ 13 The key to preparation

§ 14 Stage one: Read through

§ 15 Stage two: Blocking rehearsal

§ 16 Stage three: First run through off-book

§ 17 Stage four: Dress rehearsal

IV Common Questions and Solutions

§ 18 Analyzing questions versus giving answers

§ 19 Analyzing questions versus giving answers—Other benefits of deposition form

§ 20 Analyzing questions versus giving answers—Variations

§ 21 The physical form

§ 22 The focus swing

§ 23 Video tape deposition

§ 24 Get them on board

§ 25 English as second language; translators

§ 26 Small group preparation model

V Preparation Sessions: Step by Step Guide

§ 27 Inexperienced and experienced witnesses

§ 28 First witness preparation session with inexperienced witness; tried and don'ts

§ 29 First witness preparation session with inexperienced witness step one—Tried and do's

§ 30 Follow-up sessions with inexperienced witness

§ 31 First witness preparation session with experienced witness;

Reprinted from Westlaw with permission. Copyright 2019, Thomson Reuters. All rights reserved.

In addition to finding AM. JUR. TRIALS articles which are helpful for explaining the deposition process, look for resources that provide examples of deposition questions specific to your client's issue. Also available on Westlaw Edge is PATTERN DEPOSITIONS CHECKLISTS, which "is a comprehensive guide to depositions, providing thousands of checklists and other deposition aids for plaintiff and defendant for myriad civil litigation topics."[3]

Reprinted from Westlaw with permission. Copyright 2019, Thomson Reuters. All rights reserved.

For additional resources on **Westlaw Edge**, switch your view to *Practical Law*, and select Litigation, then Discovery & Evidence. Narrow your results by resource type or jurisdiction, or by keyword search. As you type your keywords, suggestions on related content will appear to help guide you to specific content. For example, typing in *deposition* prompted deposition. . . notice, objection, outline, preparation, questions, subpoena, witness preparation, and depositions expert.

---

[3]   Westlaw Edge scope note for DOUGLAS DANNER & LARRY L. VARN, PATTERN DEPOSITIONS CHECKLISTS (4th ed. 2018).

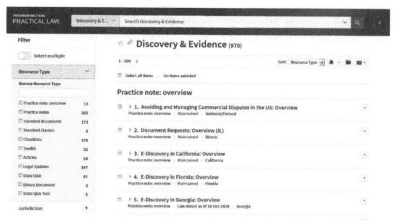

Reprinted from Westlaw with permission. Copyright 2019,
Thomson Reuters. All rights reserved.

Lexis Advance® has content organized by practice area or industry, but Civil Litigation content is available in the *Lexis Practice Advisor®* content. Selecting *Discovery* allows researchers to sort by content (checklists, forms, etc.) or by task (initial disclosures, written discovery, e-discovery, etc.).

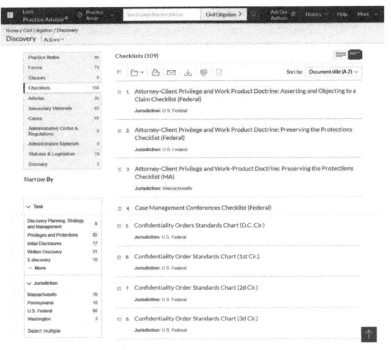

Reprinted from LexisNexis® with permission. Copyright 2019 LexisNexis®. All rights reserved.

On **Bloomberg Law,** search for *depositions* to find guidance on Depositions Checklists, Advantages and Disadvantages of Depositions, Basic Points to Consider in Depositions, and Defending Dispositions. The following screen shot[4] provides an employment overview on the Basic Points to Consider in Depositions and a brief discussion of the governing rules.

---

4   Reprinted with permission by Bloomberg Law. Copyright 2019.

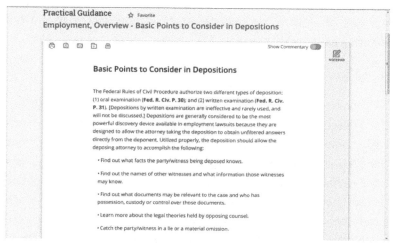

Reprinted from Bloomberg Law with permission. Copyright 2019,
the Bureau of National Affairs, Inc. All Rights Reserved.

2. Finding People

Regardless of what your client's legal issue is, you will need to find out some information from other people who are involved in your client's case. You will need to find addresses and contact information of people you plan to depose or serve, and you will probably want to learn more about someone before you meet with them. This has become increasingly easier to do, thanks to social media and the amount of personal information shared on the internet. While you can find a lot of information by Googling someone's name, a more targeted approach using a unique identifier (a Social Security Number) will provide more reliable results. In addition, some of the people you should research are professionals, such as judges, opposing counsel, and/or expert witnesses.

Some public records contain sensitive personal information, such as a Social Security Number (SSN) or a date of birth, which could cause embarrassment or harm if released to the public and not redacted. Make sure any documents you file with the court has this type of sensitive information redacted to protect yourself from violating any privacy concerns.[5]

a. *Finding Public Records*

While public records have always been available to the public, the internet makes finding digital copies of public records much easier. Public records are available for free on many government websites and for a fee through many commercial sites. Like any legal research project, when you are looking for a specific public record, look for an authoritative site. Think about which government agency would collect and store the information you are looking for before spending any money on commercial sites. Often the commercial sites offer a service of collecting all available public records in one report for a fee. Pay attention to the authoritativeness of the information—look for sites that have .gov in the domain for sources that collection information directly from individuals, over sites that appear to have a commercial interest in mind that end in .com and are collecting and compiling the information for a fee.

Public records are those records that are filed with a state or federal government entity. Additionally, publicly *available* information is not necessarily filed with a government entity, but is freely available to the public, such as telephone numbers or home addresses. Individual state statutes may define public records differently. For example, in Tennessee, public records are defined at Tenn. Code Ann. § 10-7-403:

Public records within the county shall be construed to mean:

1)   All documents, papers, records, books, and books of account in all county offices, including, but not limited to, the county clerk, the county register, the

---

[5]   For more information on protecting your client, please see Chapter 7: Ethics.

county trustee, the sheriff, the county assessor, the county mayor and county commissioners, if any;

2) The pleadings, documents, and other papers filed with the clerks of all courts, including the courts of record, general sessions courts, and former courts of justices of the peace, and the minute books and other records of these courts; and

3) The minutes and records of the county legislative body.[6]

Check the statutes that define public records in your jurisdiction. Some public records contain sensitive personal information, such as a social security number or date of birth, which could cause embarrassment or harm if released to the public and not redacted.[7] Not all records filed with the government are available to the public, including tax returns and other private records.

Google allows you to narrow your search results to a specific domain. Follow the below example if you want Google to search through only government web sites for a specific jurisdiction, such as Tennessee.

---

[6] Tenn. Code Ann. § 10-7-403 (Lexis Advance 2019).

[7] Dean Snappy, *The #1 Reason People Get Redaction Wrong*, LawSites (Oct. 10, 2019), https://www.lawsitesblog.com/2019/10/the-1-reason-people-get-redaction-wrong.html.

Example: site:.gov and "public records" and Tennessee

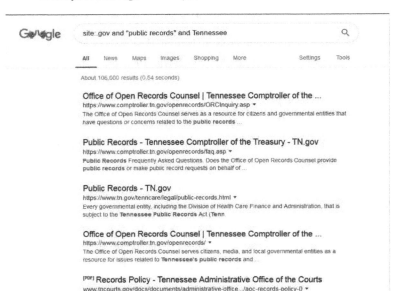

Limiting your search results will help identify the government agencies who collect public records and streamline your search to authoritative resources.

Trying to identify people through free public resources can be tricky. First, what is the correct spelling of the person's full name? A general Google search might work, or Google's Social Search Engine, Social Searcher.[8] Many people use nicknames instead of their given names, use a middle name instead of their legal first name, or have the same name as a relative. Publicly available information may not be current or complete and navigating through

---

[8]   Google Social Search searches through Facebook, Twitter, Google+, Snapchat, Linked In, and Pinterest, https://www.social-searcher.com/google-social-search/. To find additional social media search engines, look for information provided by a friendly academic librarian. Search Google for: site:.edu and "social media" and "search engines".

the free websites with inconsistent information will make your job harder.

Casetext's Tracer,[9] LexisNexis® Accurint®,[10] or Westlaw's PeopleMap[11] provide databases of public records that may be outside of your subscription plan, but might be worth a per search charge, if available. When you consider all of the various government entities who collect information and all the sources of information people create by and about themselves and others, you could spend a great deal of time on free web sites, compiling your own complete record. Alternatively, you could collect all of the information you need through one search, using a commercial resource. Think about doing a comprehensive criminal background search on an individual. You would need to check county records, state records, and federal records. Commercial public record services link all of the data collected by various state, local, and federal government entities together in **one** record. Once you find the person you are looking for, all related content is linked together. If you choose to pay for this service, the only question you need to ask is when the information was last updated.

If you are representing an individual, you have probably learned a lot about your client through what they have shared with you and the information entered on their client intake form. In addition to what you already know, you may want to research property records to verify a client's assets and find out if there are any liens or judgments against them. Believe it or not, your client may not always tell you everything you need to know, or may leave out critical information they did not consider necessary to share. It

---

[9] CASETEXT, *Public Records Search With Tracer*, https://casetext.com/public-records.

[10] LexisNexis® acquired the parent company of Accurint® in 2006. For more information on subscribing to LexisNexis Accurint® for Legal Professionals, please visit https://www.lexisnexis.com/en-us/products/accurint-for-legal-professionals.page.

[11] THOMSON REUTERS, *PeopleMap on Westlaw*, https://legal.thomsonreuters.com/en/products/people-map. PeopleMap is not available through LMU's academic license.

is never a bad idea to do some due diligence on your client. There is a wealth of information available, for free, in public records and your client intake form should have recorded their SSN. However, finding and compiling this information can often be cumbersome and time-consuming.[12]

b. *Verifying Public Records*

The hardest thing about finding information for a specific person using free resources is verifying the information you are finding is for the person you need. This can be made easier if you have a Social Security Number (a SSN is a unique identifier used by state and government entities). When you do not have an individual's SSN, it can be tricky to compile information you find on the internet for one person. There are very few unique names. Adding to the sheer mass of available data, misspellings, outdated information, and social media posts, information available on the internet can make finding correct information about a person very challenging.

I will use myself as an example. I am married and I have had two legal names. I have lived in six different states and the only social media presence I have is a LinkedIn account. However, if you Google or search through public records databases using my name, "Ann Long," you may not find the information you are seeking. My first and last name, Ann Long, are generic, and it just might drive you crazy trying to locate the information specific to me. Even using previous research suggestions such as using a search engine specifically for public records, does not always provide the

---

[12] *See generally*, CAROLE A. LEVITT & JUDE K. DAVIS, INTERNET LEGAL RESEARCH ON A BUDGET: FREE AND LOW-COST RESOURCES FOR LAWYERS (2014); CAROLE A. LEVITT & MARK E. ROSCH, THE CYBERSLEUTH'S GUIDE TO THE INTERNET: CONDUCTING EFFECTIVE FREE INVESTIGATIVE & LEGAL RESEARCH ON THE WEB (2012); CAROLE LEVITT & MARK ROSCH, FIND INFO LIKE A PRO: MINING THE INTERNET'S PUBLICLY AVAILABLE RESOURCES FOR INVESTIGATIVE RESEARCH (2011).

information you are seeking.[13] The example from Spokeo (below) finds nearly 2,000 people named Ann Long. Even narrowing the results to Tennessee still returns almost 100 records. It is not enough to know someone's first and last name, or even the city where they live. For best results, you will need a person's full name and last known address, and at least one additional piece of information, such as a phone number, approximate age, prior addresses, or known relatives or neighbors.

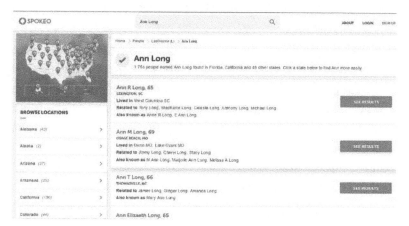

The known associates or relatives that Spokeo identifies may also be useful for conflicts checks. When you decide to represent an individual, you cannot have had any prior representations of individuals that may conflict with your current client.[14] Most law firms have a process known as a "conflict check" to verify that each

---

[13]   There are several public records search engines. 411.com, PeopleFinder.com, AnyWho.com, Intellus.com, Spokeo.com, etc. All of these sources provide various options for finding publicly available information on people. The trick is trying to discern which information is current and correct. Even after you pay a fee for the report, there is no guarantee that the information you have purchased is correct or current.

[14]   MODEL RULES OF PROF'L CONDUCT r. 5.1 cmt (AM. BAR ASS'N 2018). See also, *ABA Model Rules of Professional Conduct 1.7: Conflict of Interest, Current Clients,* https://www.americanbar.org/groups/professional_responsibility/publications/ model_rules_of_professional_conduct/rule_1_7_conflict_of_interest_current_ clients/.

new client will not be affected by the firm's past clients. If your firm has represented Wal-Mart in defending against a frivolous personal injury claim in the past, your firm will probably not represent an individual interested in suing Wal-Mart for slipping and falling in one of their stores. Regardless of the validity of the individual's claim, this would be considered a conflict of interest for the law firm and Wal-Mart will likely take their legal business elsewhere. If you are a solo practitioner or working in a small firm, you may be interested in researching databases or other services to find a solution that will help you keep track of your clients.

Locating assets can be useful in order to find a person, or to determine what a person owns (or owes!). There is not a national free database of all real property or personal property records; however, city and county property databases and tax records are available. There are also personal property databases to find the tangible and intangible property used or held for use by a business. Below are some examples of public records databases in Tennessee. Search for an equivalent entity in your jurisdiction.

- Knox County Property Tax Search[15]

- Nashville Assessor of Property[16]

- Nashville and Davidson County Personal Property[17]

- Shelby County Assessor of Property[18]

- Shelby County Personal Property[19]

Although these resources are free it is very time consuming to compile a complete and accurate record for any one individual.

---

[15] Available at https://www.knoxcounty.org/apps/tax_search/.

[16] Available at http://www.padctn.org/real-property-search/.

[17] Available at http://www.padctn.org/personal-property/.

[18] Available at https://www.assessor.shelby.tn.us/content.aspx.

[19] Available at https://www.assessor.shelby.tn.us/content.aspx?key=Personal Property.

Thankfully, verifying the data with the person you are looking for can be solved with two little things: a SSN and access to a public records database from a fee-based research service, such as Casetext's Tracer,[20] LexisNexis® Accurint®,[21] or Westlaw's PeopleMap.[22] Usually, you will know an individual's name or an address to begin your search. With fee-based public records databases, all related data is linked—aliases, addresses (current and former), assets, professional licenses, and court records (including bankruptcies and criminal records). Information linked to the same individual, regardless of misspellings, will be linked together, thanks to an unique identifier/social security number.

PUBLIC RECORDS		
GOOD	CHEAP	FAST
Public Records are available from local, state, and federal government sources via the internet.	Free.	If you know the person you are looking for, have the correct spelling of their names, or have enough information to verify the information you find.

---

[20] CASETEXT, *Public Records Search With Tracers*, https://casetext.com/public-records.

[21] LexisNexis® acquired the parent company of Accurint® in 2006. For more information on subscribing to LexisNexis® Accurint® for Legal Professionals, please visit https://www.lexisnexis.com/en-us/products/accurint-for-legal-professionals. page.

[22] THOMSON REUTERS, *PeopleMap on Westlaw*, https://legal.thomsonreuters. com/en/products/people-map. PeopleMap is not available through our academic license.

		If you are looking for specific information, like an address.
LexisNexis® Accurint® for Legal Professionals website, Accurint® will "streamline public records searches with simple, easy-to-complete search forms. Even incomplete data can return a wealth of records to help you reliably find the people and assets you seek."[23]	Contact your local LexisNexis® representative about pricing for LexisNexis® Accurint® for Legal Professionals. Request a demo and watch a tutorial from the website. LexisNexis® also offers Customer Services training and phone support.	Fee based databases increase efficiency and accuracy. Tools are provided to create reports. All related data is compiled on one individual's record from all available federal, state, and local government entities.
Casetext's Tracer and Westlaw's PeopleMap	Contact your local representatives about pricing.	Fee based databases increase efficiency and accuracy. Tools are provided to create reports. All related data is compiled on one individual's record from all available federal,

---

[23]   Id.   •

		state, and local government entities.

c. *Monitoring People*

While no one likes unfortunate surprises, everyone likes recognition for the good deeds they do. Monitor your client by setting up an alert on Lexis Advance®, Westlaw Edge, or Google and stay current with any news about your client. If you have a flat-rate subscription with either Lexis Advance® or Westlaw Edge, make sure your content includes local news sources. If your client is not a business owner, or notorious, this may not be an easy thing to do. To set up an alert on Lexis Advance® or Westlaw Edge, you will need to first find a news story that mentions the person you are going to monitor. Begin by selecting a news source and searching for your client's name. Once you have satisfactory results of the person you intended to find, hover your mouse cursor over the alarm bell to **Create an Alert**. Follow the prompts. You may also want to set up an alert on the opposing party.

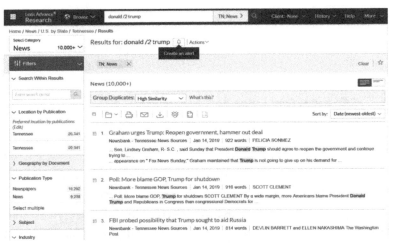

Reprinted from LexisNexis® with permission. Copyright 2019 LexisNexis®.
All rights reserved.

If you do not have local news sources included in your flat-rate contract, create and save a Google search. Go to news.google.com and create a Google account. Enter your search terms and click on *Save*, after your results display what you are looking for. Unfortunately, you will need to log in to your Google account to run your search—it will not automatically run or send you results.

3. Finding Expert Witnesses

When researching an expert witness, you are not only looking for an expert witness on a particular subject area, but also for the expert witness's litigation experience. Either you are trying to find someone who supports your position or you are researching the opposing counsel's expert and need to find holes in their record to question their credibility. Either way, your research should remain objective in order to find out as much information as you can. The goal is to learn everything you need to know about what makes the expert credible and what might make the expert less credible to a judge or jury.

a. *ALM Expert Directory*

There are several resources that can help you find and learn more about an expert witness. The ALM Expert Directory is available in print for free.[24] ALM claims to have more than 15,000 experts in their directories and offers hundreds of categories to choose from.[25] Visit their website and choose your region, and in about 2-3 weeks, a print copy should arrive. "Each book features full page resumes, a comprehensive listing section, and an extensive index that allows you to quickly identify just the right expert for your case."[26]

Once you have an expert's resume/curriculum vita, you may be able to find the full text of their articles for free from periodical databases, by searching either Google Scholar or JSTOR. Although the author's vita will list the articles they have written, it will be up to you to find the full text of those articles.[27] There is a resource that most libraries (public, academic, and law) will likely have in their reference section: FULLTEXT SOURCES ONLINE.[28] This is a two-volume set that provides an alphabetical listing of periodicals and, as you might guess, where you can find the full text of articles online. Most online databases require a subscription, but publishers often provide options to purchase individual articles.[29] A typical

---

[24] From the ALM Expert website, https://www.almexperts.com/printrequest, "Fill out the form below to receive your FREE copy of the ALM Experts Directory. Published by ALM, the ALM Experts Directory has been designed to save you valuable time and resources by providing you with direct access to the qualifications of expert witness, consultants and other litigation service providers. Each book features full page resumes, a comprehensive listing section, and an extensive index that allows you to quickly identify just the right expert for your case. Sign up below and your FREE directory will be on its way."

[25] ALM EXPERTS, https://www.almexperts.com/category/a.

[26] Id.

[27] Expert Witness databases do not include hypertext links to the author's publications.

[28] FULLTEXT SOURCES ONLINE (INFORMATION TODAY, INC. 2019) (currently a two-volume set, updated annually). For more information, visit http://books.infotoday.com/directories/fso.shtml.

[29] Most individual articles cost between $25-$35 each. This may sound expensive, but when you consider how much time you will spend trying to track down

entry will include the periodical's name, the ISSN (International Standard Serial Number), the document type (newsletter, peer reviewed, magazine, etc.), and the online databases and coverage dates. Most periodicals began appearing online in the 1990s. If you have articles that are older, you will likely need to find a library that subscribes to the print periodical and either request it through interlibrary loan, which may take weeks, or contact the publisher, which may cost money. If you have a Lexis Advance® or Westlaw Edge subscription, you may have access to an expert's article, but it may be outside of your flat-rate contract. Make sure you find out the actual cost of an article before you purchase an article outside of your contract for more than twice the actual cost![30]

Some articles are available for free while others will charge a modest per article cost. Some colleges and universities offer their graduates' access to JSTOR—visit JSTOR's website to learn more about costs and access.[31] Also check with your law school. Some law schools offer their graduates' access to HeinOnline's Law Journal Library, which provides access to a wealth of law review articles and journals your expert may have written.

b. *Lexis Advance® Context for Expert Witnesses*

Context is a relatively new feature[32] available on Lexis Advance®. This resource provides analytics on expert witness testimony and whether an expert has been persuasive to a particular

---

a free source through interlibrary loan (which may take weeks), $35 for the information you need RIGHT NOW is a bargain!

[30] According to the 2019 Westlaw Subscriber Pricing Guide, general and specialty publications are $102. Pricing is subject to change.

[31] JSTOR, https://about.jstor.org/get-jstor/.

[32] Bob Ambrogi, *"Context," Launching Today from LexisNexis, Applies Unique Analytics to Judges and Expert Witnesses*, LawSites (Nov. 29, 2018), https://www.law sitesblog.com/2018/11/context-launching-today-lexisnexis-applies-unique-analytics-judges-expert-witnesses.html.

judge.[33] Context is based on data collected from case law, not through dockets. From the LexisNexis® Context website:

> Know expert witnesses' weaknesses—before you hire one—so you can avoid a fatal addition to your litigation and trial teams. **Context for Expert Witnesses**, a new offering from the Lexis Analytics® suite, also gives you hardest-to-find facts so you can protect your witness in a Daubert challenge and undercut an opposing expert's credibility.
>
> Only Context for Expert Witnesses uses technology to **pinpoint *why* judges admitted or excluded an expert's testimony,** so you can know in advance how to select the right expert, defend their testimony or impeach opposing counsel's expert.[34]

LexisNexis® Context provides analytical data on the language used by judges and expert witnesses in case opinions. If your expert has testified, but the case settled, your expert's testimony will not be included or analyzed in Context. The only available testimony and analytical data is from cases that have been resolved by trial and where a case opinion exists. In the example below for an expert, Joseph Bond Philips, III, you can see he has been hired to testify in 112 cases, mainly for the plaintiff.

---

[33] Id.

[34] LEXISNEXIS®, *Context for Expert Witnesses: Know the Language. Protect Your Expert. Exclude Theirs.*, https://www.lexisnexis.com/en-us/products/context/expertwitnesses.page.

Reprinted from LexisNexis® with permission. Copyright 2019 LexisNexis®.
All rights reserved.

Select the *Analytics* tab to view expert challenges and the outcome. If you plan to hire Mr. Philips, the good news is that he has been hired for 112 cases and only challenged once.[35]

---

[35] While his testimony only appears in three published cases, of the potential one-hundred and twelve appearances, his testimony was challenged 33% of the time.

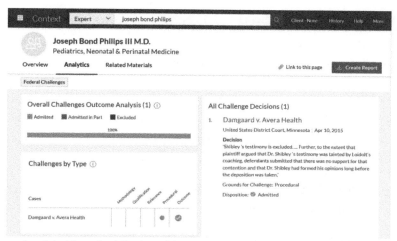

Reprinted from LexisNexis® with permission. Copyright 2019 LexisNexis®.
All rights reserved.

Selecting the *Related Materials* tab allows you to filter by Cases, Dockets, Jury Verdicts & Settlement, etc. Mr. Philips appears on 14 dockets and in 112 Jury Verdicts & Settlements reports (contact information, only).

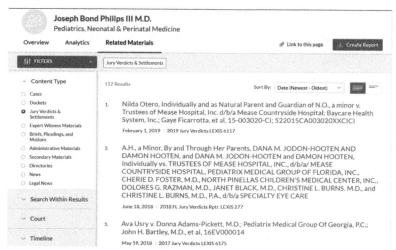

Reprinted from LexisNexis® with permission. Copyright 2019 LexisNexis®.
All rights reserved.

The information provided by Context could also be found by searching for your expert in a case law database and a careful reading of how the expert's testimony affected the outcome of the case. However, the additional information connected in Context— the Jury Verdicts and Settlements, the number of cases and case types, and the number of court appearances—all make the information in Context very worthwhile and much faster than researching and compiling information on your own.

c. *Westlaw Profiler & Thomson Reuters Expert Witness Service*

Westlaw offers a wealth of expert materials and reports on challenges, expert evaluator reports, jury verdicts and settlements, trail transcripts, and oral arguments. In addition to narrowing your search to the type of information, you can also search by jurisdiction. The screen shot from Westlaw Edge (below) shows search options:

Reprinted from Westlaw with permission. Copyright 2019,
Thomson Reuters. All rights reserved.

Searching for our expert, Joseph Bond Philips, III provides various useful data—the expert's vitae, depositions, directory information, profiles, and publications. Unfortunately, a lot of the information identified is not linked to the full text of publications or trial testimony. The Expert Evaluator Report is organized by year and notes the expert's appearance in a chart listing the dockets, opinions, and jury verdicts and also identifies the roles the expert has played (testifying for the plaintiff or defendant).[36]

Reprinted from Westlaw with permission. Copyright 2019, Thomson Reuters. All rights reserved.

The **Expert Challenge Report** identifies the case where our expert's testimony was challenged, but leads the researcher only to the case, providing no analysis or commentary (this is consistent with the information found using Context). If our expert had testified in numerous cases that all included published decisions, the chart would be helpful in identifying when his testimony was challenged to save time sorting through all decisions. However, if an expert's

---

[36] Screen shot from Westlaw Edge.

testimony is challenged often enough, the expert probably would not have many court appearances!

Reprinted from Westlaw with permission. Copyright 2019, Thomson Reuters. All rights reserved.

Thomson Reuters Expert Witness Service[37] also uses artificial intelligence to compile their results, as does Westlaw's Profiler Expert Evaluator Reports and Expert Challenges Reports. The Expert Evaluator Report provides, "a comprehensive analysis of an expert witness. The report summarizes key relationships of the expert to others utilizing case law, jury verdicts, dockets, briefs, trial documents, and expert testimony." The Expert Challenges Report tracks "challenges to the admissibility of an expert's testimony." The Thomson Reuters's website lists pricing and what is included in each report (see the image on the next page).[38] The full report contains everything from links to the expert's publications, social media activity, and Daubert challenges.[39] Before you baulk at the potential cost, consider how many hours of your time you would

---

[37] THOMSON REUTERS EXPERT WITNESS SERVICES, https://www.trexpertwitness.com/expert-background-research/ (emphasis in original).

[38] Id.

[39] Id.

need to invest to get comprehensive information, and this is only after you have identified an expert witness.

Litigation Reports				
CONTENT	EXPERT PUBLICATIONS REPORT $450	EXPERT NEWS & INTERNET ACTIVITY REPORT $450	LITIGATION GOLD REPORT $700	LITIGATION PREMIER REPORT $1,200
Links to publications by expert on Westlaw (up to 200)	✓			✓
Links to publications citing expert on Westlaw (up to 200)	✓			✓
Links to publications by expert from other online sources (up to 20)	✓			✓
Westlaw news links (up to 200 most recent)		✓		✓
Up to 3 pages internet research for internet profiles, activity, blogs, video, and other postings		✓		✓
License and certification verification		✓		✓
Court documents: Up to 150 court document links from Westlaw			✓	✓
TREWS challenge report: 10 years			✓	✓
Westlaw Evaluator report			✓	✓
Five full-text documents			✓	✓
	ORDER REPORT >	ORDER REPORT >	ORDER REPORT >	ORDER REPORT >

Reprinted from Westlaw with permission. Copyright 2019, Thomson Reuters. All rights reserved.

Expert Witness Resources		
GOOD	CHEAP	FAST
ALM Experts	Free. ALM Experts offer a free regional print directory on request. Helpful for identifying expert witnesses on any particular issue.	Print copy will arrive in the mail in 2-3 weeks.
LexisNexis® Context	Contact your LexisNexis® representative for pricing. Expert	Contact 888-ATLEXIS

Westlaw Profiler or Thomson Reuters Expert Witness Service	witness information compiled from published case law. Prices range for a full report that includes docket and case law research.	Contact 877-468-9536

4. Judges

It is easy to find information about people who want to be found, especially if those people are also elected officials. Considering that 38 states[40] elect a portion of their judges, you will probably be able to find out a lot of information on your judge without a lot of effort. Begin with the court's website and the judge's biography to learn the correct spelling and full name of your judge. Next, search for cases decided by your judge and news article written about his or her decisions.[41]

a. *Almanac of the Federal Judiciary*

If you are looking for a federal judge, the ALMANAC OF THE FEDERAL JUDICIARY[42] is a good place to begin. It is available on Westlaw Edge or available in print in most academic and federal court law

---

[40] AMERICAN BAR ASSOCIATION, *Fact Sheet on Judicial Selection Methods in the States*, https://www.americanbar.org/content/dam/aba/migrated/leadership/fact_sheet.authcheckdam.pdf.

[41] When searching for people, enter their firstname /2 lastname to broaden your search to include any middle initials or names and use the appropriate advanced search field to narrow your search to only those people who are judges (in this example). On Westlaw Edge, JU(dale /2 drozd) and on Lexis Advance®, JUDGE(dale /2 drozd).

[42] From the scope note on Westlaw Edge, the "Almanac of the Federal Judiciary contains biographical information on currently-serving federal judges, including U.S. Supreme Court justices, circuit court judges, district court judges, magistrates, and bankruptcy court judges. This material also includes media coverage and anonymous lawyers' evaluations." Also available online through Wolters Kluwer.

libraries. Let's begin our search with a judge in the Eastern District of California, Hon. Dale Drozd. His profile begins with biographical information, but the reason you would use this resource is to gain insight from lawyers who have appeared before Judge Drozd and insights from his clerks in the "lawyers' evaluation" section. This entry, from the Almanac of the Federal Judiciary available on Westlaw Edge, also provides the correct pronunciation of the judge's name, explaining that Drozd rhymes with rose.

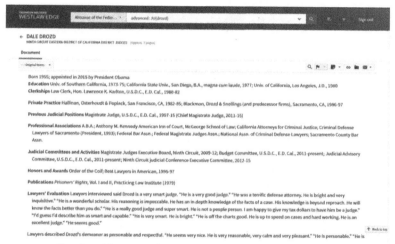

Reprinted from Westlaw with permission. Copyright 2019, Thomson Reuters. All rights reserved.

b. *Westlaw Edge's Litigation Analytics*

It is even easier to find information about your judge if you can take advantage of artificial intelligence (AI) that creates a report on the outcomes of your judge's decisions. Westlaw Edge's Litigation Analytics offers an extensive analysis into the decision patterns of state and federal judges. Begin your search in a Westlaw Edge case law database. Select the advanced search option and enter the name of your judge in the judge's field (this will focus your results on only those cases that have been decided by your judge). Open any of the cases you find and hover your mouse over the judge's name and a pop-up box will appear, prompting your to *See Full Profile*. Follow this link to view the judge's profile, references, and reports.

Reprinted from Westlaw with permission. Copyright 2019, Thomson Reuters. All rights reserved.

The *Appeals Analytics* can be used to determine how often a judge has been reversed. This report can be sorted by Case Type, Result (positive, mixed outcome, negative, or other), Judge, Law Firm, Attorney, or Date. There are also analytics on Outcomes, Motions, Precedent, Expert Challenges,[43] Appeals, and References (links to cases decided, any secondary sources that discuss your judge or his or her decisions, dockets and links to judicial directories that contain biographical information).

---

[43] From the Westlaw Overview, "An Expert Challenge Report provides information derived from litigation in which an expert witness was challenged for admissibility. Expert Challenge Reports are available for experts and for judges who rules on the challenge."

c. Fastcase's Docket Alarm

Fastcase recently acquired Docket Alarm, an "analytics tool for identifying judicial trends and predicting litigation outcomes."[44] Docket Alarm provides "analytical profiles on judges, parties, law firms, and attorneys, identifying win rates, time to decision" and more.[45] If you have access to Fastcase through your state bar membership, you can add a subscription to Docket Alarm for $99/month or choose a pay-as-you-go option.[46] Although some of the most impressive (and beautiful!) features are designed for patent and trademark practice, you can also search federal, state, and county court dockets. You won't find any biographical data, but you can learn a lot about how your judge is likely to rule on any given case type.

Begin searching by judge:drozd and narrow by court—California Eastern District Court. The results will provide you with the total number of cases Judge Drozd has heard, (22,938!), the case types heard most often (prisoner's civil rights—4,510), and the attorneys who have argued before Judge Drozd the most often (see the screenshot from Docket Alarm on the next page). Docket Alarm allows you to export this data to an Excel spreadsheet, which allows you to further sort and analyze the data. Docket Alarm offers an Analytics Workbench that allows users to create their own analytics for any court for a separate subscription.[47]

---

[44] *Fastcase Provides New Competitive Advantage with Litigation Alerts and Legal Analytics Through Docket Alarm Addition* (Jan. 10, 2018), https://www.fast case.com/press/fastcase-expands-legal-analytics-capabilities-with-docket-alarm-acquisition/.

[45] Id.

[46] DOCKET ALARM, *Hassle Free Pricing*, https://www.docketalarm.com/pricing.

[47] Id. Our academic license does not include the Analytics Workbench.

d.   *LexisNexis® Context*

Looking at the results we have from Docket Alarm, we may be interested in learning more about Judge Drozd. LexisNexis® Context® provides analytical information on published cases and is searchable by either Judge or Expert Witness.[48] LexisNexis® Context uses AI to analyze the language used in court decisions and is intended to help lawyers write more persuasive motions.[49] The Overview provides biographical information (education, experience, and contact information), which you could also find on the court's website. Also included in the Overview are the number of Opinions By Area of Law (civil procedure = 5,066) and Opinions by Year (close to 500 cases every year!). These statistics may help paint a clearer picture of the judge's caseload, but there is no real data about the time a case may take from initial filing to the final disposition because the data Context® analyzes is based on published case opinions only—not the corresponding docket information. Selecting

---

[48] LEXISNEXIS®, *Context*, https://www.lexisnexis.com/en-us/products/context. page.

[49] LEXISNEXIS®, *Context for Judges: Know the Language, Write a More Persuasive Motion*, https://www.lexisnexis.com/en-us/products/context/judges.page.

the Analytics tab leads to more granular information about Motion Language and Citation Patterns. However, considering that Judge Drozd's caseload is dominated by prisoner right's cases involving civil rights issues (which we learned from Docket Alarm), and the motion filed most often is a Motion to Dismiss, more digging is necessary. The blue FILTERS option helps narrow the scope of results by Motion Type, Keyword, or Practice Area displayed in the screen shot from LexisNexis® Context (below).

Reprinted from LexisNexis® with permission. Copyright 2019 LexisNexis®. All rights reserved.

e. *Fastcase and Google*

If you do not have access to Fastcase's Docket Alarm, LexisNexis®'s Context, or Westlaw Edge's Litigation Analytics, you will have to compile this information on your own. Fastcase and Google Scholar do not have the option to narrow your case law research by limiting your search terms to appear in specific field for the judge's name. However, Google Scholar does have an author search option that will identify the judge as the "author" of the case. If we needed to compare Judge Drozd's decisions without the help of AI, let's compare the results of our initial data set.

From the other biographical resources, we have learned that Judge Drozd's full name is Dale Alan Drozd and he is a judge in the California Eastern District Court (federal).

Service	Search Query	Number of results
Westlaw Edge (California Federal District Courts)	JU(dale /2 drozd) Dale /2 drozd	3,209 3,406
Lexis Advance® (California Federal District Courts)	Judges(dale /2 drozd) Dale /2 drozd	5,203 5,358
Fastcase 7 (California Eastern District Court)	"judge dale a. drozd" dale /2 drozd	207 4,527
Google Scholar (Eastern District of California)	author:dale /2 drozd "judge dale a. drozd" judge /3 drozd dale /2 drozd	42 501 6,140 8,290

Comparing the results from all five initial datasets, we can agree that Judge Drozd has decided somewhere in the neighborhood of 42 to more than 5,000 cases. We can narrow these results to practice area or topic on Lexis Advance® and Westlaw Edge, but not on Fastcase or Google Scholar (again, low-cost and free services do not allow searching by field, so it makes sense that narrowing by topic or practice area would also not be available). All services will allow the researcher to narrow the initial dataset with additional keywords (contract, civil rights, pensions, etc.) or by date of decision.

The point of this little exercise is to demonstrate how much time AI can save, even though it will initially cost more than a free search on Google Scholar. However, there is no guarantee that AI will produce perfect results. Depending on what you are looking for, an imperfect data set may provide you with the gist of what you need. If perfection is what you are seeking, you may need to use more than one research service.

5. Finding Public and Private Business and Corporate Information

If you are representing a business, you will need to do some research on the key personnel, the corporate structure, and the company's financials. There are a lot of information resources available for publicly traded companies, because people invest in public companies and the Securities and Exchange Commission (SEC) requires companies to be transparent with their investors. All of this information is filed on EDGAR[50] (the Electronic Data Gathering, Analysis, and Retrieval system). EDGAR provides public access to company filings and

> . . .performs automated collection, validation, indexing, acceptance, and forwarding of submissions by companies and others who are required by law to file forms with the U.S. Securities and Exchange Commission (SEC). Its primary purpose is to increase the efficiency and fairness of the securities market for the benefit of investors, corporations, and the economy by accelerating the receipt, acceptance, dissemination, and analysis of time-sensitive corporate information filed with the agency.

---

[50] U.S. SECURITIES AND EXCHANGE COMMISSION, https://www.sec.gov/edgar.shtml.

If this is your first time conducting corporate research, visit the EDGAR website and read through the Quick EDGAR Tutorial.[51] The SEC's website also provides an explanation on the type of information you can find in the various required forms. There is an explanation on How to Read a 10-K,[52] the required annual report, which describes the company's business, any potential or perceived risks, and an overview of the company's operating and financial results for the past fiscal year.

If you are representing a private company, begin by searching for the company's website.[53] Most company websites are created for marketing purposes, but you can usually learn where the company is physically located, the industry, and possibly the names of the key personnel you will need to meet or depose. However, the content on a company's website is created by the company and you may need to do a bit more research to verify any claims. Additionally, at the first sign of trouble, some company's may pull down their website. The Internet Archive can help you find company websites, or any other deleted or replaced web content, with the Wayback Machine. Use the company's website to find their current URL (Uniform Resource Locator). There is only one option for searching the Wayback Machine archived content, with a URL.

---

[51] U.S. Securities and Exchange Commission, Quick EDGAR Tutorial, https://www.sec.gov/edgar/quickedgar.htm.

[52] U.S. Securities and Exchange Commission, How to Read a 10-K, https://www.sec.gov/fast-answers/answersreada10khtm.html.

[53] Additionally, Forbes keeps track of America's Largest Private Companies at https://www.forbes.com/largest-private-companies/list/. The list can be sorted alphabetically by company name or size and provides links to the company's website, the state where the company is located, the industry, the annual revenue, and the number of employees.

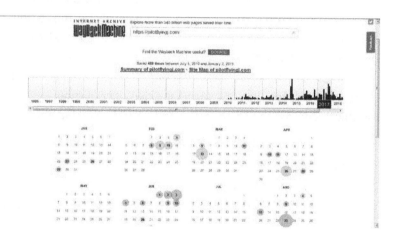

Private companies are not required to file any documentation with the SEC, which makes learning the financial status of a private company (or any other information they do not intend to make public) somewhat difficult. For more tips on researching private companies, turn to a corporate librarian who has compiled a list of resources for their patrons in a LibGuide. For example, to find LibGuides on private company research using Google, search:

site: libguide: researching private companies

This will quickly lead you to numerous LibGuides on the subject. This also helps focus your search on the type of results you actually want—LibGuides—and not all of the distracting news stories or competing advertisements attempting to divert your attention.

For additional research on public or private companies, begin with Dun & Bradstreet, if you have access to this subscription database. If not, try a company directory on Lexis Advance®, Westlaw Edge, or Bloomberg Law. On Lexis Advance®, Locate a Business in the Public Records database, or search LexisNexis® Corporate Affiliations™ to find information on corporate hierarchy and additional information about both public and private corporations. The following screen shot is for a private company,

Pilot Corporation, headquartered in Knoxville, Tennessee, from LexisNexis® Corporate Affiliations™.

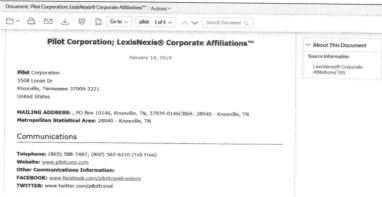

Reprinted from LexisNexis® with permission. Copyright 2019 LexisNexis®. All rights reserved.

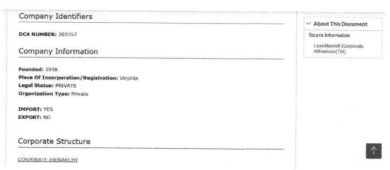

Reprinted from LexisNexis® with permission. Copyright 2019 LexisNexis®. All rights reserved.

Executives

Officers:

OFFICER	TITLE TYPE	ROLE(S)	EMAIL/SOCIAL MEDIA
Dan Fleming, VP-Ops	Executive	Administration/Operations Vice President	EMAIL: FlemingD@pilotcorp.com LINKEDIN: www.linkedin.com/pub /dan-fleming/12/55b/300

Download Table

Description

Pilot Corporation was founded in 1958, and is based in Knoxville, TN. It is a gas station chain. The stations amenities include restaurants, parking facilities, truck washing, maintenance, and repair services. It also includes check cashing, money transfer, laundry, shower, and game rooms. Its partners include IMTA, KMTA, TMTA, and PMTA and others.

Reprinted from LexisNexis® with permission. Copyright 2019 LexisNexis®. All rights reserved.

Industry Type: Truck Stops & Convenience Stores Operator

Market And Industry

NAICS Codes:
447190 - Other Gasoline Stations
445120 - Convenience Stores
SIC Codes:
5541 - Gasoline Service Stations
5411 - Grocery Stores
Competitors:

Holiday Companies
QuikTrip Corporation

Reprinted from LexisNexis® with permission. Copyright 2019 LexisNexis®. All rights reserved.

Service Firms

Auditor: PricewaterhouseCoopers, 800 S. Gay St., Ste.1600, Knoxville, TN, 37929-1600, (865) 524-4000
Legal Counsel: Hodges, Doughty & Carson ▾, 617 Main Ave., Knoxville, TN, 37902, (865) 546-9611

Classification

Subject: GAS STATIONS (88%); RESTAURANTS (87%)

Company: **PILOT** CORP (91%%)

LexisNexis® Corporate Affiliations™
Copyright 2019 LexisNexis, a division of Reed Elsevier Inc. , All Rights Reserved

Reprinted from LexisNexis® with permission. Copyright 2019 LexisNexis®. All rights reserved.

However, the type of directory information found in resources such as LexisNexis® Corporate Affiliations™, will not provide you with any information on whether a company is or has been involved in litigation. For this information, you will need to access the litigation analytics from a service that offers company information.

a. *Bloomberg Law Company Litigation Analytics*

Currently, only Bloomberg Law provide litigation analytics for companies. Using Bloomberg Law, select Litigation Analytics (from the *Law School Success* page, under *Practice Tools*). Search for your company's name[54] to view that company's litigation history (and so much more!).[55]

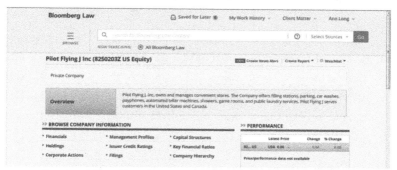

Reprinted from Bloomberg Law with permission. Copyright 2019,
the Bureau of National Affairs, Inc. All Rights Reserved.

Scroll down to learn more about a company's financial picture and litigation history.[56]

---

[54] Before you begin your litigation search, know the exact name (and correct spelling) of the company you are researching. Searching Bloomberg for "Pilot" results in dozens of company names. Wikipedia is pretty good at providing the correct spelling of well-known public and private companies, and it's free.

[55] Reprinted with permission by Bloomberg Law. Copyright 2019.

[56] Reprinted with permission by Bloomberg Law. Copyright 2019.

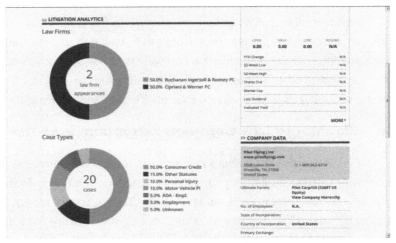

Reprinted from Bloomberg Law with permission. Copyright 2019,
the Bureau of National Affairs, Inc. All Rights Reserved.

Click on the *Case Types* graphic to launch the litigation
analytics and access more information on the law firms and profiles
of the attorneys who have represented the company, the
jurisdictions where your company has been sued, the various case
types, and a litigation history chart that displays how often your

company is sued. Scroll down to view the individual case dockets, as shown in the screen shot below.[57]

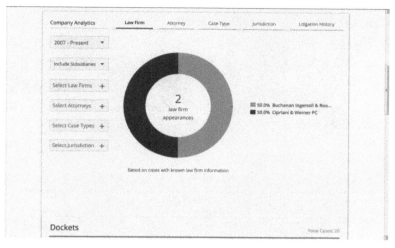

Reprinted from Bloomberg Law with permission. Copyright 2019, The Bureau of National Affairs, Inc. All rights reserved.

---

[57] Reprinted with permission by Bloomberg Law. Copyright 2019.

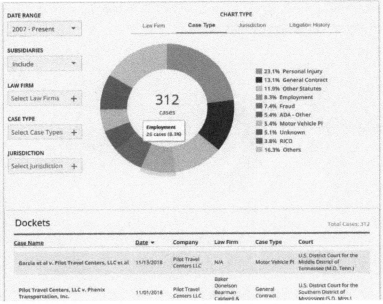

Reprinted from Bloomberg Law with permission. Copyright 2019,
The Bureau of National Affairs, Inc. All rights reserved.

CHAPTER 5

Litigation Phase III: Pretrial Action Finding Pleadings, Motions, and Briefs

The pretrial stages of civil litigation generally include the continuation of discovery, pretrial hearings, conferences, and the filing of pleadings, briefs, and motions. By this stage you are already familiar with the applicable laws, your court's rules, your client and opposing party, the judges, and how often issues similar to your client's are successful. If you are solo, or practicing in a small firm, you may not have access to a data management system with scads of motions and/or forms that can be modified to fit the needs of your client. However, you do have access to motions that have been filed with all federal courts and those state courts that have an electronic case management system (ECM). The real trick here is to find a motion you can modify for your client's legal issue and this is where artificial intelligence (AI) can help. There are several research services that pull data from PACER and other state ECMs and provide a relatively easy method to identify relevant pleadings, briefs, and motions. Alternatively, at the end of the chapter are additional resources for pleadings, briefs, motions, and forms available in print at your local law library, or through legal research services.

1. Federal and State Court Electronic Dockets

Large law firms have brief banks stocked with sample clauses and pleadings that new associates can use as a starting point to modify for their individual client's needs. In addition, lawyers can also access a wealth of pleadings, motions, and forms through legal research services. Relatively new are research services that use artificial intelligence (AI) to identify legal authorities that may have been overlooked. These research services scan an uploaded document for the legal issues they discuss, verify whether the cases cited are still "good" law, and provide additional case law on point with the legal issues presented.

Most legal documents include portions of boilerplate language[1] used by attorneys over and over again. For example, if you are drafting a motion for summary judgment,[2] you will likely use the exact same language contained in Rule 56, "the movant shows that there is no genuine dispute as to any material fact and the movant is entitled to judgment as a matter of law"[3] and possibly the language cited in the 1986 U.S. Supreme Court decision, *Celotext Corp.*, "[s]ummary judgment is appropriate when the moving party shows that the record—the admissions, affidavits, answers to interrogatories, declarations, depositions, or other materials—is without a genuine issue of material fact and that the moving party

---

[1]   "Ready-made or all-purpose language that will fit in a variety of documents." *Boilerplate*, BLACKS' LAW DICTIONARY (11th ed. 2019).

[2]   Jim Wagstaffe, *Making the Motion for Summary Judgment (Federal)*, LEXIS PRACTICE ADVISOR J. (Nov. 2, 2018), https://www.lexisnexis.com/lexis-practice-advisor/the-journal/b/lpa/posts/making-the-motion-for-summary-judgment-federal-2130606407.

[3]   FED.R.CIV.P. 56.

is entitled to judgment as a matter of law."[4] Of course this language will be modified slightly to address your client's issues, but unless the rule or the law changes, this portion of the motion will remain the same and can be copied and pasted into any motion for summary judgment. No need to recreate the wheel, which is why brief banks and databases containing motions and forms are so very valuable to the practice of law.

If you can find a motion or pleading on point with your client's legal issue, it can be edited to conform to your client's individual needs and may not require you to start from scratch, which saves you a lot of time that would otherwise be billed back to the client. One fairly inexpensive[5] place to begin looking is PACER,[6] although your search options are limited. PACER (Pubic Access to Court Electronic Dockets) is easiest to use when you know a specific party name or docket number. Almost all federal courts[7] (excluding the U.S. Supreme Court) and many state courts[8] have an electronic docket. Lawyers and non-lawyers alike can create a PACER account and search for specific federal court documents and related information.

> Public Access to Court Electronic Records (PACER) is an electronic public access service that allows users to obtain case and docket information online from federal appellate, district, and bankruptcy courts, and the PACER Case Locator. PACER is provided by the Federal Judiciary

---

[4]   Celotext Corp. v. Catrett, 477 U.S. 317 (1986).

[5]   *Electronic Public Access Fee Schedule*, PACER, https://www.uscourts.gov/services-forms/fees/electronic-public-access-fee-schedule; *see also* Debra Cassens Weiss, *PACER Should Be Free, According to Amicus Brief by Posner and 6 Other Retired Judges*, ABA J. (Feb. 4, 2019), http://www.abajournal.com/news/article/pacer-should-be-free-according-to-amicus-brief-by-posner-and-six-other-retired-judges.

[6]   PUBLIC ACCESS TO COURT ELECTRONIC RECORDS (PACER), https://www.pacer.gov/.

[7]   Access to specific federal court dockets is available on PACER, https://www.pacer.gov/psco/cgi-bin/links.pl.

[8]   The National Center for State Courts maintains a list of public and private access to state court dockets at https://www.ncsc.org/topics/access-and-fairness/privacy-public-access-to-court-records/state-links.aspx.

in keeping with its commitment to providing public access to court information via a centralized service.[9]

After you create a PACER account, download the browser extension RECAP. The mirror image of PACER is RECAP and a mirror image is exactly what RECAP attempts to do.[10] "RECAP is an online archive and free extension for Firefox and Chrome that improves the experience of using PACER, the electronic public access system for the U.S. Federal District and Bankruptcy Courts."[11] The RECAP browser extension will identify when a PACER document has already been purchased from PACER by a kind soul who has then added the document to the RECAP repository for others to enjoy at no cost. The browser extension will turn blue when the document is available in RECAP and a little blue R icon will appear next to PACER documents.

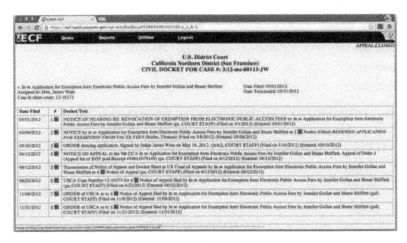

If you have the RECAP[12] browser extension, any document you view while you are logged on to PACER will automatically be uploaded to RECAP. Similarly, any document that has already been

---

[9]   PACER, https://www.pacer.gov/.

[10] RECAP, https://free.law/recap/.

[11] Id.

[12] RECAP is PACER spelled backwards.

uploaded to RECAP is publicly available for free and will also have the blue R RECAP icon next to the document link:

Follow the RECAP icon to view the document for free. You will receive a prompt letting you know your document is available from RECAP and then get redirected to the Court Listener website to view and download the document.

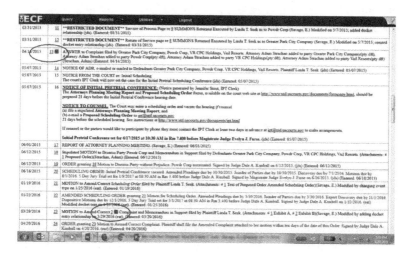

RECAP is only available or federal district and bankruptcy dockets and only works with the Firefox or Chrome browsers.

If you are looking for state and county court dockets, the National Center for State Courts provides a list of state electronic court management systems.[13] The coverage and accessibility varies by state. For example, in Tennessee, only two county dockets are

---

[13] NAT'L CTR. FOR STATE COURTS, *Electronic Filing: State Links*, https://www.ncsc.org/Topics/Technology/Electronic-Filing/State-Links.aspx.

currently online, Shelby and Davidson. Visit your state or county's court website to learn more about what is available.[14] Alternatively, if you have access to a legal research service, you can search all available state ECMs through Bloomberg Law's Docket Search, Fastcase's Docket Alarm, Lexis Advance®'s CourtLink®, or Westlaw's State Dockets.

In addition to the wealth of documents available through docket research services, all of the information entered into the fields of the docket sheet are also available for searching (party names, judge, attorney or law firm, civil or criminal, nature of suit, cause of action, and date).[15] All of this information can be compiled and analyzed by data type and provide you with a wealth of specific data on the court system you file in. Although all of this data has been available for years, it would take several hours for a human to sort through all of the information and create something meaningful.[16] This is where artificial intelligence makes all of this data much more manageable and easier to navigate.

There are options to search by Nature of Suit (NOS) and Cause of Action (COA), but on PACER, the result list provides only the docket number and party names for all matching cases. This may be enough to lead you to something relevant, if you can find a plaintiff or defendant in the same industry, for example. Let's pretend you represent a client who lives in Florida and was injured while videotaping her granddaughter taking a ski lesson at Park City

---

[14] "In addition to providing information about the status and procedural history of an appeal, you will be able to directly access all motions, orders, judgments and opinions filed in the appellate courts after August 26, 2013". TENNESSEE COURTS.GOV PUBLIC CASE HISTORY, https://www.tncourts.gov/courts/supreme-court/public-case-history.

[15] "The PACER Case Locator (PCL) is a national index for district, bankruptcy, and appellate courts. The PCL serves as a search tool for PACER, and you may conduct nationwide searches to determine whether or not a party is involved in federal litigation. Each night, subsets of data are collected from the courts and transferred to the PCL." PACER COURT LOCATOR, https://pcl.uscourts.gov/pcl/index.jsf.

[16] Actually, this is the sort of thing law librarians and paralegals were asked to do for large law firms decades ago. Solo practitioners may not have access to a librarian, but now they have the option to purchase litigation analytics.

Mountain Resort in Utah.[17] If you are looking for similar cases with related motions and pleadings, you would begin your PACER search with what you know: the Cause of Action is 28 U.S.C. 1332 (diversity jurisdiction, personal injury) and Nature of Suit is 360 (other personal injury). Searching PACER for all related cases in the Utah Federal District Court will lead you to lots (hundreds) of results. However, you can quickly browse through the cases and find similar defendants, such as the ski areas of Powder Mountain, Snowbird, etc. Once you find a docket on point with your issue, the next step is browsing through the dockets to find successful outcomes for plaintiffs, and then modifying the pleadings to match your client's facts. The docket research services available through Bloomberg Law's Docket Search, Fastcase's Docket Alarm, Lexis Advance®'s CourtLink®, or Westlaw's State Dockets allow keyword searching, which will make your research process much easier.

2. Dockets and Litigation Analytics

PACER began in the late 1990s and revolutionized the practice of federal litigation.[18]

> Lawyers speak of reduced stress at a workday's end, knowing they can electronically file a document until midnight, without fear that the courthouse doors will close on them. In clerks' offices, work has changed from filing and stamping papers to performing quality control to make sure electronic entries are accurate and up to date. And everyone, from a self-represented litigant to an

---

[17] This is a real case, *Seek v. Vail Resorts, Inc.*, No. 2:15cv-00187 (U.S.D.C. Utah Feb. 13, 2018).

[18] UNITED STATES COURTS, *25 Years Later, PACER Electronic Filing Continue to Change Courts* (Dec. 9, 2013), https://www.uscourts.gov/news/2013/12/09/25-years-later-pacer-electronic-filing-continue-change-courts.

appellate judge, can track cases and case documents in nearly real time.[19]

With nearly three decades of data, the current release of litigation analytics available through commercial legal research services further revolutionizes the practice of law. All of the data entered on the cover sheet to the final court document filing is now available for searching and analyzing.

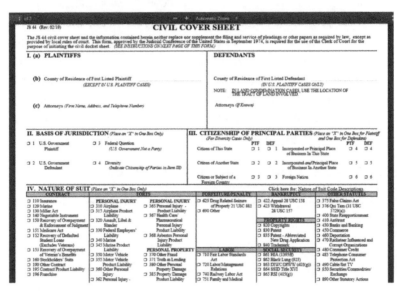

However, a lot of this data is either incomplete (missing pages!) or incorrect (typos!). In addition, a lot of court documents are filed by pro se litigants and written by hand (often illegible).[20] Commercial vendors are "normalizing" some of this data to give researchers more confidence in their results.[21]

---

[19]   Id.

[20]   For example, in the U.S. District Court of Colorado, 20% of civil cases were filed by pro se litigants. Kristen L. Mix, Pro Se Litigation: A View From the Bench, THE BENCHER: AM. INNS OF COURT (Jul/Aug. 2017), https://home.innsofcourt.org/AIC/AIC_For_Members/AIC_Bencher/AIC_Bencher_Recent_Articles/2017_JulAug_Mix.aspx.

[21]   A LexisNexis® handout explains how "attorney-editors work hand in hand with the courts to identify, clarify and correct substantive factual and legal errors in

Using the fact pattern from above, you may have learned that there are a handful of law firms (or attorneys) who represent ski areas. Once you have identified these firms/lawyers, you could search by attorney name or law firm name and then narrow by NOS, COA, etc. However, due to the imperfect nature of PACER, you should not expect perfection in your search results. For example, law firm mergers create new law firm names, but the cases tried before the merger may not be found if the researcher is only searching by law firm name (either current or prior). If that same researcher searched using an attorney's name instead, and that attorney worked at both the former and the current law firm, the results would provide a more comprehensive data set. Additionally, it may be difficult to find complete results when a researcher uses the word "and" in a law firm's name when that firm uses an ampersand between named partners, such as Hunton & Williams. One of the law firms I used to work for, Hunton & Williams, recently merged with Andrews Kurth, creating a new firm named Hunton Andrews Kurth.[22] While it is important to recognize the data you find using litigation analytics are filed in an imperfect system (PACER), depending on what you are trying to accomplish, you may not need perfect results.[23] If you are looking for motions and pleadings from a specific law firm or attorney, be diligent with your research starting point because your research results may differ if you begin searching for a law firm vs. searching for an attorney.

---

cases. . . Case-law editors examine cases for format problems, incorrect citations, case-name errors and other issues. Editors make needed corrections to improve searching, citation recognition and results." Handout on file with the author.

[22] Thanks to my former boss, Frosty Owen, for sharing this news. Brenda Sapino Jeffreys & Christine Simmons, *It's Official: Andrews Kurth and Hunton & Williams Will Merge*, LAW.COM (Feb. 21, 2018), https://www.law.com/texaslawyer/2018/02/21/its-official-andrews-kurth-and-hunton-williams-will-merge/?slreturn=20190714211954.

[23] At the 2019 American Association of Law Libraries Annual Meeting, a panel of librarians evaluated legal analytics and compared the strengths and weaknesses of each system. Zach Warren, *Law Librarians Push for Analytics Tools Improvements After Comparative Study*, LAW.COM (Jul. 15, 2019), https://www.law.com/legaltech news/2019/07/15/law-librarians-push-for-analytics-tools-improvement-after-comparative-study/?slreturn=20190713091856.

Using a research service to search dockets instead of PACER will likely improve the accuracy of your search results because the data may have been normalized to improve results.

a. *Fastcase's Docket Alarm*

Docket Alarm provides "analytical profiles on judges, parties, law firms, and attorneys, identifying win rates, time to decision" and more.[24] If you have access to Fastcase through your state bar membership, you can add a subscription to Docket Alarm for $99/month or choose a pay-as-you-go option.[25] Although some of the most impressive (and beautiful!) features are designed for patent and trademark practice, you can also search federal, state, and county court dockets. Let's pretend you are a lawyer in Oregon and a potential client comes to your office seeking your advice on filing a sexual orientation discrimination claim against her employer. Oregon is one of a few states that provide additional protections to its citizens who suffer from discrimination based on their sexual orientation beyond what federal law provides. This is the first time you have worked on this type of case and you would like to find a complaint filed in an Oregon court with similar facts. Begin by selecting your court and entering your search terms (discrimination and "sexual orientation" in Oregon County Courts) (see the Docket Alarm screen shot on the following page).

---

[24] Id.

[25] DOCKET ALARM, *Hassle Free Pricing*, https://www.docketalarm.com/pricing.

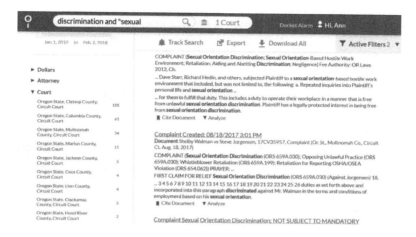

In the screen shot above, filtering your results to include Pleadings provides 321 results to browse through. Other ways to narrow your results are by Dollars, Attorney, Court, Judge, Status, Party, or Type. Filtering by Status (Closed) and Type (Contract) further narrows our results to 12 complaints. Selecting any of the complaints will take you to the actual complaint and highlight the relevant language where your search terms appear:

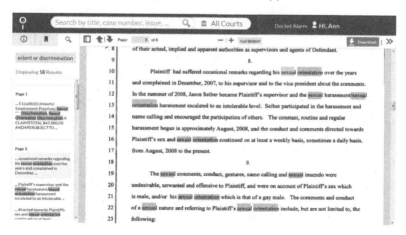

As you can see, you could quickly browse through the 12 complaints to find something you could begin to modify for your client's particular facts.

b. *Bloomberg Law's Litigation Analytics*

If you have access to Bloomberg Law, you also have access to federal district court and select state dockets through the Litigation Analytics feature. Bloomberg is the only research service offering litigation analytics searchable by company name. Using our earlier example involving a ski accident at Park City, Utah, you could begin your search using the company name. Very quickly we learn that Park City Mountain Resort is owned by Vail Resorts, Inc. Just typing "Vail" in the main search box leads you to a link for more information about the company, including their litigation history:[26]

Reprinted from Bloomberg Law with permission. Copyright 2019, The Bureau of National Affairs, Inc. All rights reserved.

Following the COMPANIES link to Vail Resorts, Inc. provides an astonishing amount of additional information that would take hours to compile. However, the Litigation Analytics feature pulls together

---

[26] Reprinted with permission by Bloomberg Law. Copyright 2019.

all related information in seconds, and includes a company profile, corporate hierarchy, recent company news, and the litigation history of the company is chock full of additional information to make our job of finding related pleadings much easier.[27]

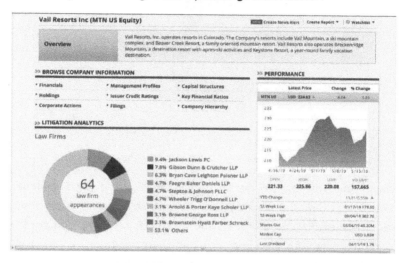

Reprinted from Bloomberg Law with permission. Copyright 2019,
The Bureau of National Affairs, Inc. All rights reserved.

In the Litigation Analytics section, narrow by Case Type (a.k.a. the Nature of Suit option in PACER) to find pleadings related to the other thirty-five cases where Vail has had to defend against personal injury lawsuits (although Vail Resorts has 84 court appearances, only 35 were filed as personal injury lawsuits).[28]

---

[27] In PACER, you can only search one jurisdiction at a time and there is really no easy way to find where similar cases have been filed against the same company. Reprinted with permission by Bloomberg Law. Copyright 2019.

[28] Reprinted with permission by Bloomberg Law. Copyright 2019.

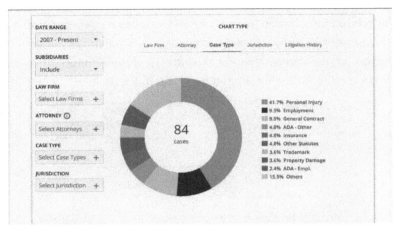

Reprinted from Bloomberg Law with permission. Copyright 2019,
The Bureau of National Affairs, Inc. All rights reserved.

Narrowing further to the 10th Circuit Court (which includes Colorado, Utah, and Wyoming, all states with large ski resorts) will identify pleadings filed in the same jurisdiction, to help you quickly find pleadings with the same issue and court heading. With 25 cases available, it wouldn't take long to browse through the available dockets[29] to find what you need.

---

[29]   Reprinted with permission by Bloomberg Law. Copyright 2019.

Dockets					Total Cases: 25
Case Name	Date ▼	Company	Law Firm	Case Type	Court
Baup v. Vail Summit Resorts	02/03/2017	Vail Summit Resorts Inc	Wheeler Trigg O'Donnell LLP Bryan Cave Leighton Paisner LLP/US	Personal Injury	U.S. Court of Appeals for the Tenth Circuit (10th Cir.)
Brigance v. Vail Summit Resorts	01/30/2017	Vail Summit Resorts Inc	Bryan Cave Leighton Paisner LLP/US	Personal Injury	U.S. Court of Appeals for the Tenth Circuit (10th Cir.)
Graves v. Lagasse	01/19/2017	Vail Resorts Inc	N/A	Personal Injury	U.S. District Court for the District of Colorado (D. Colo.)
Peterson et al v. Vail Resorts Inc	07/25/2016	Vail Resorts Inc	N/A	Personal Injury	U.S. District Court for the District of Wyoming (D. Wyo.)
Homayounfar v. The Vail Corporation	09/28/2015	The Vail Corp Vail Resorts Inc	N/A	Personal Injury	U.S. District Court for the District of Colorado (D. Colo.)
Brigance v. Vail Corporation, The	06/30/2015	The Vail Corp Vail Summit Resorts Inc	N/A	Personal Injury	U.S. District Court for the District of Colorado (D. Colo.)
Baup v. Vail Summit Resorts, Inc.	03/27/2015	Vail Summit Resorts Inc	Wheeler Trigg O'Donnell LLP	Personal Injury	U.S. District Court for the District of Colorado (D. Colo.)
Seek v. Vail Resorts et al	03/23/2015	Greater Park City Co	N/A	Personal Injury	U.S. District Court for the District of Utah (D. Utah)
		Vail Resorts Inc			U.S. District Court for the

Reprinted from Bloomberg Law with permission. Copyright 2019,
The Bureau of National Affairs, Inc. All rights reserved.

The company information allows you to create a news alert, a watch list, a custom or a quick report on the company—all of which will save a lot of time and keep you up-to-date on any information that may impact your client's case. If you are a plaintiff's lawyer, you will want to learn as much as possible about the law firm and attorneys who are likely to represent Vail. Knowing the attorney's names will help you do further research on who you will be up against and allow you to conduct further research on their litigation history for other clients and in other courts. The Litigation Analytics allow you to view the law firms and attorneys who have represented Vail in the past and narrow to only those case types (NOS) similar to your client. All of this is easy to do in Bloomberg, and doesn't incur any additional charges. Additionally, Bloomberg allows you to search the full text of the docket entries by keyword, which is not available on PACER.

Once you have identified a docket on point with your client's issue, you have access to all the related pleadings filed in PACER (sadly, RECAP does not integrate with Bloomberg's dockets). Now you have a motion or pleading you can use as a starting point. Modify the pleadings to fit your client's issue(s) and make sure any cases or statutes cited in the pleadings are still good law and (obviously) on point with your client's issue.

3. Artificial Intelligence

A quick and easy way to update the research in your motion or pleading is to employ AI. There are several options to choose from—Casetext's CARA AI[30] or ROSS Intelligence,[31] to name a few.[32] Upload your brief to identify any leading case law you may have missed and make sure the cases you have cited are still good law. The ROSS Document Analyzer will scan an uploaded document and look for cases to identify whether any of your cited cases have received any negative treatment. ROSS Intelligence is similar to what LexisNexis® and Westlaw have offered for decades, and at $69 per month, is only slightly cheaper than Lexis Advance® or Westlaw Edge and doesn't offer near the content.[33]

a. Casetext's CARA AI

Casetext has been around since 2013 and has been gaining momentum and popularity with law schools and law firms ever since. In a nutshell, Casetext's CARA AI is a research tool that "reads" a complaint or brief that has been uploaded and identifies case law authorities that discuss the same legal issues in your

---

[30]   Casetext is available at https://casetext.com/. Casetext won the American Association of Law Libraries New Product of the Year award in 2017.

[31]   ROSS, https://intercom.help/ROSSIntelligence/en/articles/2039688-document-analyzer.

[32]   At Lincoln Memorial University Duncan School of Law, we provide our students and faculty with educational subscriptions to Casetext and Ross Intelligence. BriefCatch is not available for Mac users and Judicata's Clerk currently provides California state law only.

[33]   ROSS, https://rossintelligence.com/pricing.html. See also, *Using Shepard's BriefCheck on Lexis Advance*, https://www.lexisnexis.com/pdf/lexis-advance/using-shepards-briefcheck.pdf; *Westlaw Edge Quick Check*, https://legal.thomsonreuters.com/en/products/westlaw/edge/quick-check.

jurisdiction—in *seconds!*[34] Here's an example, using the complaint from the *Seek* case filed in the Utah District Court:

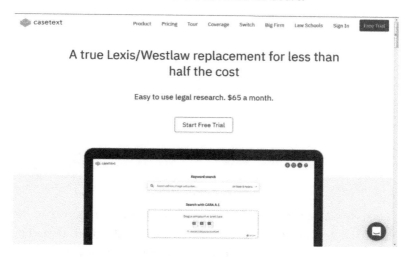

After uploading the complaint, I added the keywords "personal injury" and ski!, narrowed by jurisdiction to the 10th Circuit, and removed all unpublished cases and cases already cited in the complaint. Casetext's CARA AI has identified additional cases that may be on point with my issue. There are options to narrow this initial set of cases by District Court, motion type, Cause of Action, Party Type, and/or Date. There is also an option to search within this set of cases for additional keywords.

---

[34] *Artificial Intelligence Is As Easy As Drag and Drop,* https://casetext.com/product.

Like all legal research tasks, now the researcher must read the cases and decide if there are additional cases that would strengthen the legal argument. The Casetext CARA AI's strength is in the ability to analyze an entire document, not just a search query of keywords. Although I did add the additional keywords of "personal injury" and ski!, the top cases cited all involve ski resorts, and did not interpret my root expander to include skill, or skin, or any other word that begins with the root of "ski."

What law students and new associates find most frustrating about legal research is the combined lack of research expertise and knowledge of a legal issue to craft an excellent Boolean Logic search string. Although research is the best way to learn about a legal issue, not fully understanding the legal issue from the beginning can lead to what is often perceived as "wasted" time. For law students and new associates, being able to start a project with a document on point with their legal issue may provide the shortcut necessary to streamline the learning process and result in a legal document of higher quality. Casetext's CARA AI may be one way solo and small law firm practitioners can compete with the expertise of large law firm lawyers who have mentors and brief banks readily at their disposal. If you have not yet written a brief, you could find a similar case that addresses your issue by cutting and pasting the headnotes into a "brief."

Westlaw offers a Brief It feature that allows researchers to create a brief from an existing case. After you have found a case on point, select the Brief It button.

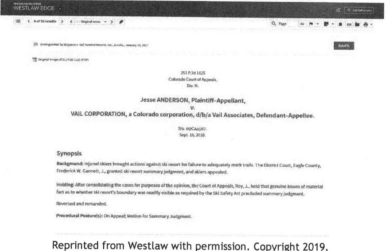

Reprinted from Westlaw with permission. Copyright 2019, Thomson Reuters. All rights reserved.

The Brief It feature then extracts the West Headnotes into a "brief" that can be saved and uploaded to CARA. If you have access to Lexis Advance®, you can cut and paste the headnotes into a "brief." The Lexis Advance® headnotes are generated by an algorithm and are the actual language from the court's decision. The Westlaw Edge Headnotes are created by West Editors and may not include the actual language from the court's decision.

Reprinted from Westlaw with permission. Copyright 2019,
Thomson Reuters. All rights reserved.

Uploading the Westlaw Brief into CARA and cutting and pasting some of the key words from the forth West Headnote, *"ski area operators" and duty and "ski area boundaries"* CARA finds an additional seven cases for our review that were not cited in the Westlaw "Brief."

Selecting the link to one of the legal issues below the language from the court's decision, *Tort—Failure to Warn*, narrows this list to two cases, and provides an additional legal issue, *Agency— Premises or Supervisor Liability*, and a Motion for Summary Judgment.

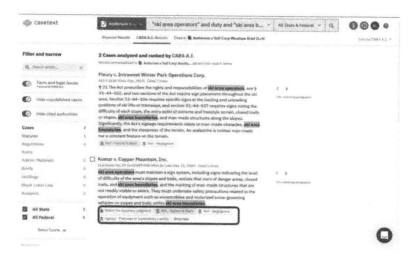

Make sure you upload your document to Shepard's® BriefCheck™ to verify that the laws you have cited are still "good law" or individually check your cites for any negative treatment using Shepard's® (Lexis Advance®), KeyCite (Westlaw Edge), BCite (Bloomberg Law), or BadLawBot (Fastcase).

b. *The Future of AI: Judicata's Clerk*

Good news for California lawyers—Judicata's Clerk may be the most cost-efficient solution for evaluating the strength of your motions. Sadly, it is currently only available for California state law. However, what Judicata provides is a glimpse of how powerful AI could be to the practice of law.

The founder of Judicata's Clerk describes it as "moneyball for motions."[35] You begin by uploading a brief to Clerk. Clerk runs through an analysis that compares your brief to "thousands of pages of legal text and millions of case data points in order to place each brief in context and provide actionable insights."[36] Your brief is then graded by the strength of your argument, drafting skills, context, and given an overall grade.[37]

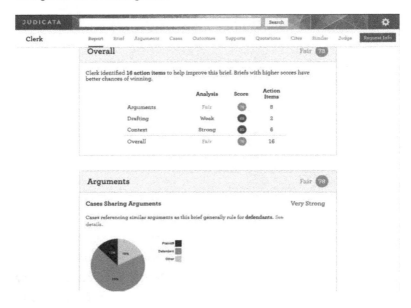

---

[35] Jean O'Grady, *Forget the Robots You Might Just Need a Clerk. Judicata's Clerk: Algorithms and Analytics That "Grade" and Recommend Edits to Briefs.*, DEWEY B STRATEGIC (Nov. 10, 2017), https://www.deweybstrategic.com/2017/11/judicata-clerk.html. *See also* https://www.judicata.com/demo/clerk/report.

[36] Id.

[37] Id.

Vulnerability of Cited Cases   Weak

A **significant** number of the cases cited in this brief may be **highly vulnerable** to attack. See details.

Outcomes of Cited Cases   Weak

This brief addresses more plaintiff-winning cases than defendant-winning cases. This may indicate that the brief is not presenting enough favorable defendant-winning precedent. See details.

Breakdown of Supporting Cases   Strong

This brief supports **many** of its principles with on-point precedent. Six principles in this brief may have stronger supporting cases, either as replacements or string cites. See details.

Drafting   Weak

Breakdown of Quotations   Very Poor

This brief does a **very poor** job of correctly citing and attributing quotations. In this brief, **seven quotations** from California cases and statutes are incorrect. See details.

Breakdown of Citations   Good

This brief does a **good** job of correctly citing cases. In this brief, **six citations** to California cases are incorrect. See details.

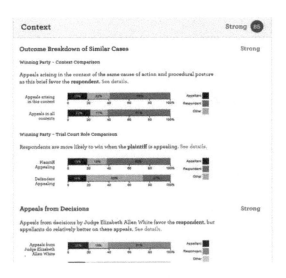

If you plan to practice in California, visit Judicata's website to see a demo and learn more about the functionality. Clerk goes far and beyond compiling data and actually provides additional insights into the strengths and weaknesses of your brief. Judicata's Clerk would be very worthwhile to solo and small law firms, just as soon as they expand to other jurisdictions.

The Ethics of Online
Legal Research

Legal research and writing are the skills every practicing lawyer relies on to be successful, but every practicing lawyer also needs to be aware of the ethical issues associated with legal research. This chapter will explore the ethical duty lawyers have to their clients while conducting legal research online.

1. Competence

In today's environment, an attorney's *online* legal research skills must be competent and thorough. ABA Model Rule 1.1 imposes a duty of competence upon all lawyers and defines competent representation to include "the legal knowledge, skill, thoroughness and preparation reasonably necessary for the representation."[1] Because conducting research is often an essential part of the "thoroughness and preparation reasonably necessary for the representation," this ethical component applies directly to legal research.

---

[1] MODEL RULES OF PROF'L CONDUCT r. 1.1 cmt. 8 (AM. BAR ASS'N 2018). This rule has been around since 1983!

The idea of competent and diligent legal research is not new. Numerous lawyers have faced professional discipline or judicial sanctions for failing to conduct competent research in the course of representing a client.[2] In a Supreme Court of Colorado decision from 2009, *People v. Maynard,* the attorney was suspended from the practice of law for one year for poor research and for filing a frivolous lawsuit.[3] In concluding the attorney lacked the competence to file her RICO claim, the court specifically cited the attorney's "lack of meaningful legal research." The court observed, "[r]espondent had been practicing law for 16 years when she filed her RICO suit, yet none of her research included cases decided between 1996 and June 2003."[4]

Rule 11 of the Federal Rules of Civil Procedure is designed to prevent the filing of frivolous claims. It also imposes a duty to conduct "a reasonable investigation of the facts and a normally competent level of legal research" before an attorney certifies to the court that the filing is not frivolous.[5] However, a lawyer's failure to predict a court's ultimate resolution of an issue is generally protected from liability under the "informed judgment rule" (a.k.a., the "error in judgment rule").[6] Under this rule, there is no tort liability for an honest error in judgment concerning a doubtful or debatable point of law, provided the attorney has first undertaken reasonable legal research "in an effort to ascertain

---

[2]   *See* Oracle Am., Inc. v. Google Inc., No. C 10-03561 WHA, 2011 WL 3443835, at *5 (N.D. Cal. Aug. 8, 2011) ("Google also has not shown why diligent legal research would not have revealed this issue sooner. Google's motion for leave "to provide further elaboration" of its Section 101 invalidity contentions is Denied."); Max Sound Corp. v. Google, Inc., No. 14-CV-04412-EJD, 2017 WL 4536342, at *9 (N.D. Cal. Oct. 11, 2017) ("To the extent that Max Sound believed it could join Vedanti as an involuntary plaintiff under Rule 19, reasonably diligent legal research would have revealed that this was not an option."); Northwestern Nat. Ins. Co. v. Guthrie, 1990 WL 205945, *2 (N.D. Ill. 1990); Oxfurth v. Siemens A.G., 142 F.R.D. 424, 427-28 (D.N.J. 1991).

[3]   People v. Maynard, 238 P.3d 672, 685 (Colo. 2009).

[4]   Id.

[5]   Id.

[6]   Biomet Inc. v. Finnegan Henderson LLP, 967 A.2d 662, 668 (D.C.2009).

relevant legal principles and to make an informed decision as to a course of conduct based upon an intelligent assessment of the problem."[7] The key takeaway is this: lawyers need to conduct competent legal research.

Today's lawyers also need to understand whether litigation analytics and/or AI will be cost and time efficient for their client's issue in order to be both competent and thorough. Today's lawyers need to recognize the importance of how technological advances impact legal research related to their practice. As any law librarian can attest, staying current with legal research tools is a full time job! Every year new content and features are added to legal research services. A lawyer's duty of competence now includes a duty regarding technology, which includes new legal research technologies.[8] Lawyers must "keep abreast of changes in the law and its practice, including the benefits and risks associated with relevant technology."[9] Thirty-six jurisdictions have adopted an "ethical duty of technology competence"[10] as part of their rules of professional conduct, and Florida and North Carolina now require specific technology Continuing Legal Education (CLE) credits.[11] While there is not a consensus on what "technology" is—it can range from using email to creating smart contracts—conducting legal

---

[7] Smith v. Lewis, 13 Cal.3d 349, 359 (1975).

[8] *Supra*, note 1.

[9] MODEL RULES OF PROF'L CONDUCT r. 1.1 cmt.8 (AM. BAR ASS'N 2018).

[10] Robert Ambrogi has been tracking this trend since 2012 on his blog, LawSites, at https://www.lawsitesblog.com/tech-competence. The Florida Bar was the first to make a change to their professional responsibility rules when the Florida Supreme Court amended their rule on minimum continuing legal education standards, 6-10.3, ". . .a lawyer should engage in continuing study and education, including an understanding of the risks and benefits associated with the use of technology." *In re: Amendments to Rules Regulating the Fla. Bar 4-1.1 & 6-10.3*, 200 So. 3d 1225 (Fla. 2016).

[11] Jennifer Wondracek, Law Students—Avoid Malpractice and Embrace Technology!, ABA For Law Students Before the Bar Blog (Feb. 20, 2019), https://aba forlawstudents.com/2019/02/20/law-students-avoid-malpractice-and-embrace-technology/.

research online requires an understanding of the associated risks to your clients.

Historically, conducting legal research involved understanding how to navigate large library collections—in print. Today, most law students conduct legal research using a computer, not a book, and further, most academic law library collections have more digital titles than print titles.[12] Over several decades, online content has expanded. In the 21st century, online legal research has become the norm rather than the exception. Today, online legal research is generally considered to be more economical in both time and expense than conducting legal research using print materials.[13] A competent legal researcher should be able to conduct research using a computer and have a general knowledge of the types of information available in a digital format to support their practice.[14] However, the majority of today's practicing attorneys[15] attended law school long before legal research courses allowed full access to Lexis Advance® or Westlaw Edge during the first semester. The belief at the time was law students should learn the process of legal research using print resources before learning how to navigate the hypertext links embedded in online resources. This practice,

---

[12] An article published in 2003 discussed the findings of an ABA survey from 2001 on the "feasibility and viability of the digital library" and concluded that while a digital library is feasible, the "barriers" are the associated costs and the "attachment" to print. Catherine Sanders Reach, David Whelan & Molly Flood, *Feasibility and Viability of the Digital Library in a Private Law Firm*, 95 LAW LIBR. J. 369 (2003). A more recent article quotes an academic law library director, Pauline Aranas, Director of the Law Library and Adjunct Professor of Law at the University of Southern California Gould School of Law, explains, "[w]e are all shifting from primarily print to primarily digital collections." Pauline Aranas, et al, *"Nowhere to Run; Nowhere to Hide": The Reality of Being a Law Library Director in Times of Great Opportunity and Significant Challenges*, 107 LAW LIBR. J. 79 (2015).

[13] "The theory is that computer research reduces the amount of attorney time required for legal research and, therefore, saves the client money." *Okla. Natural Gas Co. v. Apache Corp.*, 355 F. Supp. 2d 1246, 1260 (N.D. Okla. 2004).

[14] MODEL RULES OF PROF'L CONDUCT r. 1.1 cmt.8 (AM. BAR ASS'N 2018).

[15] PRACTICEPANTHER, *2016 U.S. Lawyer Demographics Infographic*, https://www.practicepanther.com/blog/2016-us-lawyer-demographics/ (the average age of lawyers is 49 and nearly a third are between the ages of 45-54, which means most lawyers likely attended law school in the 1990s).

coupled with the fact that only a small percentage of law schools require more than one legal research course, has resulted in the majority of practicing lawyers having to learn how to conduct online legal research in practice, which can be expensive for both lawyers and their clients. Although legal research is not a subject on any state bar exam, understanding how to conduct cost effective legal research is every lawyer's ethical duty. This has created a need for CLE seminars on how technology and legal research intersect.[16]

Competent lawyers are now expected to be aware of the pitfalls of technology and understand the associated benefits and risks.[17] Related to legal research, this includes acknowledging the potential risks involved in using cloud-based services, understanding how to prevent the inadvertent or unauthorized disclosure or access to client information, and determining whether research services that utilize litigation analytics and/or artificial intelligence are necessary for practice.

2. Cloud-Based Services and Third Party Vendors

According to a 2018 Legal Technology Survey Report conducted by the American Bar Association (ABA), 54.6% of survey respondents reported using some form of cloud-based service.[18] The report defines cloud, "cloud computing," and cloud-based services as software hosted off-site, or accessed over the internet as opposed to software saved and accessed directly from a computer.[19] The

---

[16] In 2019, I have presented seven CLEs on legal research and technology to city, county, and nationwide audiences. By comparison, I am usually asked to present bi-annually. Access to the LibGuide I refer CLE attendees to can be found at http://library.lmunet.edu/legalresearchcle. The password is CLE. To access my general two-credit hour CLE, *Legal Research in an Artificially Intelligent World*, go to LawPracticeCLE at https://lawpracticecle.com/courses/legal-research-in-an-artificially-intelligent-world-self-study/.

[17] MODEL RULES OF PROF'L CONDUCT r. 1.1 cmt. 8 (AM. BAR ASS'N 2018).

[18] ABA, *2018 Cloud Computing Tech Report*, https://www.americanbar.org/groups/law_practice/publications/techreport/ABATECHREPORT2018/2018Cloud/.

[19] Id.

survey discusses cloud-based software used for storing documents, such as CLIO, Google Docs, or Dropbox.[20] However, research services that store legal authorities cited in litigation documents should also be of concern. ABA Model Rule 3.3(a) requires that

> (a)   A lawyer shall not knowingly. . .
>
>> (2)   fail to disclose to the tribunal legal authority in the controlling jurisdiction known to the lawyer to be directly adverse to the position of the client and not disclosed by opposing counsel. . .[21]

Although this rule discusses legal authorities that a lawyer *knowingly omits* from their representation, the failure to know about all relevant legal authorities suggests a lack of competent and diligent legal research. This, in turn, implicates ABA Model Rule 1.1, which, as discussed, requires that "[a] lawyer shall provide competent representation to a client. Competent representation requires the legal knowledge, skill, thoroughness and preparation reasonably necessary for the representation."[22]

a. *Data Breaches*

While a violation of a jurisdiction's rules of professional conduct may result in disbarment, evidentiary and procedural rule violations may result in litigation. Competent legal research is intended to provide the lawyer with various legal authorities to support their client's claim and inform them of any adverse decision. Often, lawyers make annotations to the legal authorities they find, either for their own reference or to share with an associate. If you have a contract with a legal research service, you have the option to save research to a folder and identify research

---

[20]   Id.

[21]   MODEL RULES OF PROF'L CONDUCT r. 3 (AM. BAR ASS'N 2018).

[22]   MODEL RULES OF PROF'L CONDUCT r. 3 (AM. BAR ASS'N 2018).

sessions by client code or client matter number.[23] While these features help to streamline billing, reduce duplication, and organize your research, the information contained in or the labeling of these research folders may include material information related to the litigation strategy for your client. Additionally, research services also allow the insertion of notes, annotations, or attorney work product of the exact language cited in a legal authority.

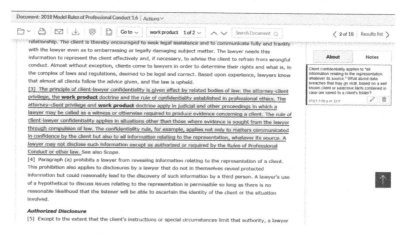

A lawyer's work product and litigation strategy is protected by work product rule contained in Rule 26 of the Federal Rules of Civil Procedure:

> (3) *Trial Preparation: Materials.*
>
> (A) Documents and Tangible Things. Ordinarily, a party may not discover documents and tangible things that are prepared in anticipation of litigation or for trial by or for another party or its representative (including the other party's attorney,

---

[23] The large law firms I worked in always used a unique multi-digit client code, followed by a unique multi-digit client matter number. If a file was left in a conference room or near a photocopier, no one would immediately identify the client matter number 35467-32019 as the Jones Divorce file. Similarly, the naming of online legal research folders should follow your firm's internal billing policies and not be clearly identifiable to a specific client.

consultant, surety, indemnitor, insurer, or agent). But, subject to Rule 26(b)(4), those materials may be discovered if:

(i) they are otherwise discoverable under Rule 26(b)(1); and

(ii) the party shows that it has substantial need for the materials to prepare its case and cannot, without undue hardship, obtain their substantial equivalent by other means.[24]

If your legal research service experiences a data breach,[25] a client's litigation strategy may be compromised and the "lawyer's ability to perform the legal services for which the lawyer is hired is significantly impaired by the episode."[26] The ABA issued a Formal Opinion on a lawyer's obligation to their client, which provides some guidance in the event of a data breach.[27] ABA Formal Opinion 483 explains,

Data breaches and cyber threats involving or targeting lawyers and law firms are a major professional responsibility and liability threat facing the legal profession. As custodians of highly sensitive information, law firms are inviting targets for hackers. . .While lawyers must make reasonable efforts to monitor their technology resources to detect a breach. . .the potential for an ethical violation occurs when a lawyer does not undertake reasonable efforts to avoid data loss or to detect cyber-

---

[24] FED. R. CIV. PRO. 26(b)(3).

[25] LexisNexis® experienced a data breach in 2013. Byron Acohido, *LexisNexis Breach Reveals "Secret Questions"*, USA TODAY (Sept. 27, 2013), https://www.usa today.com/story/cybertruth/2013/09/27/lexisnexis-breach-reveals-secret-questions/2884625/.

[26] ABA Comm'n on Ethics & Prof'l Responsibility, Formal Op. 483, p.3 (2018).

[27] ABA Comm'n on Ethics & Prof'l Responsibility, Formal Op. 483 (2018) (discussing a lawyer's obligation after an electronic data breach or cyberattack).

intrusion, and that lack of reasonable effort is the cause of the breach.[28]

When the data breach occurs to a third-party vendor the lawyer has contracted with, the lawyer is obligated to communicate the breach to clients "[i]n sufficient detail to keep clients 'reasonably informed' and with an explanation 'to the extent necessary to permit the client to make informed decisions regarding the representation.' "[29] It is possible that a data breach could result in the unauthorized access to confidential client information or an attorney's work product.[30]

b. Email

In addition to research services experiencing potential data breaches, email sent directly from a research service has the potential of not being secure. Legal research services make it easy to send statutes, cases, or any other legal documents via email. Along with the document, the lawyer may add an explanatory note. Lawyers need to be careful not to include explanatory notes that contain confidential or material information when sending documents directly from a research service. In a 2017 formal opinion, the ABA advised,

> A lawyer generally may transmit information relating to the representation of a client over the internet without violating the Model Rules of Professional Conduct where the lawyer has undertaken reasonable efforts to prevent

---

[28] Id.

[29] Id. *citing* MODEL RULES OF PROF'L CONDUCT r. 1.4 (AM. BAR ASS'N 2018).

[30] Christine Simmons, Xiumei Dong & Ben Hancock, *How Vendor Data Breaches are Putting Law Firms at Risk*, LAW.COM (Oct. 17, 2019), https://www.law.com/2019/10/17/how-vendor-data-breaches-are-putting-law-firms-at-risk/?slreturn=20190920 182515; Christine Simmons, Xiumei Dong & Ben Hancock, *Law Firm Cybersecurity: See Which Law Firms Reported a Data Breach*, LAW.COM (Oct. 15, 2019), https://www.law.com/2019/10/15/here-are-law-firms-reporting-data-breaches/ ("...reports from more than 100 law firms—searchable here—but cybersecurity experts warn that far more firms are falling victim.").

inadvertent or unauthorized access. However, a lawyer may be required to take special security precautions to protect against the inadvertent or unauthorized disclosure of client information when required by an agreement with the client or by law, or when the nature of the information requires a higher degree of security.[31]

The formal opinion addresses two concerns related to email communications. First, lawyers should be aware that email may not be a secure method of communication.

> . . .cyber-threats and the proliferation of electronic communications devices have changed the landscape and it is not always reasonable to rely on the use of unencrypted email. For example, electronic communication through certain mobile applications or on message boards or **via unsecured networks** may lack the basic expectation of privacy afforded to email communications.[32]

Second, lawyers "should understand and use electronic security measures to safeguard client communications and information."[33] The formal ethics opinion advises lawyers to use secure internet connections or a Virtual Private Network (VPN) to protect their clients from the inadvertent or unauthorized disclosure of client information.[34] Having access to a subscription research service may feel secure, until the lawyer chooses to send research related to a client's representation via email over an unsecured network.

---

[31] ABA Comm, on Ethics and Prof'l Responsibility, Formal Op. 477R (2017) (discussing securing communication of protected client information).

[32] Id. (emphasis added).

[33] Id.

[34] Id.

3. Preventing the Inadvertent or Unauthorized Disclosure of Client Information

ABA Model Rule 1.6 "governs the disclosure by a lawyer of information relating to the representation of a client during the lawyer's representation of the client. . ." and "the lawyer's duty not to reveal information relating to the lawyer's prior representation of a former client."[35] Lawyers are required to take "reasonable" efforts to prevent the unauthorized access to client information.[36] However, in an increasingly online world, data security measures need to be considered. With online legal research, lawyers need to be aware of the lack of privacy for internet or Wi-Fi access in public locations, including courts.

Our smart devices have the potential to collect, retain, and share a significant amount of personal information about ourselves and the people we interact with.[37] Think about how often you connect to unsecured Wi-Fi networks (Starbucks, hotels, etc.). Usually the knowledge that you are on an unsecured network may restrict your internet activity (for example, you may decide not to log in to your bank account and check your balance, if you know the network is not secure).[38] However, even when using a secure internet connection, the agreements signed with third-party vendors (Facebook, Verizon, etc.), may inadvertently authorize those companies to share personal data with other companies, or

---

[35] MODEL RULES OF PROF'L CONDUCT r. 1.6 (AM. BAR ASS'N 2018).

[36] Id., at (d).

[37] Kathryn McMahon, Note, *Tell the Smart House to Mid Its Own Business! Maintaining Privacy and Security in the Era of Smart Devices*, 86 FORDHAM L. REV. 2511, 2515 (2018).

[38] Lee Rainie, *The State of Privacy in Post-Snowden America*, PEW RESEARCH CENTER (Sept. 21, 2016), pewresearh.org.

the agreement to opt out of any data sharing agreement may be nullified during software upgrades.[39]

In determining whether a lawyer has made the "reasonable efforts to prevent the inadvertent or unauthorized disclosure of, or unauthorized access to, information relating to the representation of a client" the following factors may be relevant:

- the sensitivity of the information,

- the likelihood of disclosure if additional safeguards are not employed,

- the cost of employing additional safeguards,

- the difficulty of implementing the safeguards,

- and the extent to which the safeguards adversely affect the lawyer's ability to represent clients (*e.g.*, by making a device or important piece of software excessively difficult to use).[40]

Another factor you should consider when conducting online research is the search engine you use for non-legal or general research. Most folks use Google for all of their research, whether personal or related to their clients. However, you may want to consider that Google makes most of its money from ad revenue[41] targeted to users who freely submit information about themselves via the keywords entered into Google searches. "In 2018, Google's ad revenue amounted to almost 116.3 billion US dollars."[42] Google

---

[39] *See* In re Vizio, Inc., Consumer Privacy Litig., 238 F. Supp. 3d 1204, 1233 (C.D. Cal. 2017) (consumers believed they had opted out of Vizio's data collection practices, but Vizio was still collecting and sharing their data).

[40] MODEL RULES OF PROF'L CONDUCT r. 1.6 cmt. 18 (AM. BAR ASS'N 2018).

[41] J. Clement, *Google's Ad Revenue From 2001 to 2018 (in billion U.S. Dollars)*, STATISTA (Apr. 29, 2019), https://www.statista.com/statistics/266249/advertising-revenue-of-google/.

[42] Id.

has no way of discerning whether the words you type into the Google search box are associated with you, your client, or someone else.

For example, if you have a family law practice and a client is filing for divorce after learning their spouse has recently given them a sexually transmitted disease (STD), you may be inclined to Google the STD to learn more about it. If you research the STD with Google, Google will later use this information (attached to you) and give it to their ad revenue partners who will push ads about at-home STD test kits, medications for the STD, and other related products or services along with the results of your next Google search. If your computer screen can be seen by clients or others in your office, this could be embarrassing! Although there are ways to manage the amount of information Google tracks about you,[43] you could instead use a "search engine that doesn't track you," such as DuckDuckGo.com.[44] You may also want to consider installing a privacy screen on your monitor.[45]

4. Reasonable Fees

Rule 1.5 of the ABA Model Rules of Professional Conduct requires a lawyer to charge only a reasonable fee. In assessing the reasonableness of a fee, courts and disciplinary authorities consider a host of factors, including "the time and labor required, the novelty and difficulty of the questions involved, and the skill requisite to perform the legal service properly."[46] Therefore, the lawyer who bills a client for basic research in order to get up to speed on a legal issue that a competent lawyer could be expected to already understand or who bills a client for research that could have been

---

[43] David Neild, *All the Ways Google Tracks You—And How to Stop It*, WIRED (May, 27, 2019), https://www.wired.com/story/google-tracks-you-privacy/.

[44] Visit https://duckduckgo.com/ to learn more.

[45] Brett Nuckles, *Laptop Privacy Filters: What to Look For and Why You Need One*, BUS. NEWS DAILY (Jun. 6, 2018) https://www.businessnewsdaily.com/10859-laptop-privacy-filters-buying-advice.html.

[46] MODEL RULES OF PROF'L CONDUCT r. 1.5(a) (AM. BAR ASS'N 2018).

performed more easily or cheaply may be found to have charged an unreasonable fee.

A competent legal researcher should be aware of the costs involved with computer-assisted legal research. A 1993 ABA Ethics Opinion focused on the recovery of those costs.[47] Prior to 1993, online legal research was a financial boon for many law firms. Law firms that subscribed to either LexisNexis® or Westlaw would pay a monthly fee for access to those services. Law firms would then bill their clients for any associated legal research costs accrued during the month, which is completely expected and ethical. However, some law firms were charging clients a percentage on top of the actual cost the law firm was paying to LexisNexis® or Westlaw, or "padding" their bills, to cover other costs of print materials in the library. These egregious billing practices were referred to as "Skaddenomics," after one of the large firms who charged their clients more than the actual cost of the associated fees.[48] The mid-1990s were a pivotal point in law firm economics. Computers were on most desktops and this increased investment in technology also increased the need for competent support staff.[49] Until the 1993 Ethics Opinion, law firms were able to defray some of these costs by billing excessive fees for online legal research back to their clients.

In November 2018, a Canadian judge asked, "why is there a legal research fee for case precedents which are available for free

---

[47] *Supra*, note 4.

[48] Susan Beck & Michael Orey, *Skaddenomics*, Am. Law., Nov. 1991, at 3, available at amlawdaily.typepad.com/files/skaddenomics.pdf (detailing how corporate law firms turned every aspect of client representation into a profit center).

[49] Albert L. Moses, *Technology; Warning! Fixed Fees Ahead (Engage All Systems)*, 21 L. PRACTICE MANAGEMENT 60 (March 1995) (discusses the introduction of computers into the practice of law and the need for lawyers to become technologically skillful).

through CanLII or publically accessible websites?"[50] The judge went on to say,

> $900.00 for legal research is problematic. One assumes that counsel graduated with the basic legal knowledge we all possess. This matter was unlikely his first blush with the world of "occupier's liability", and specifically the liability of landlords. Counsel no doubt was familiar with the focus on the degree or control and access exercised by the landlord on the subject area. So given all the base experience and knowledge, the need for "research" by some anonymous identity is questionable.[51]

Building on this ethics opinion, several courts have classified electronic research as firm overhead, not costs that can be recouped from clients.[52] Today, more law firms discount or absorb legal research costs rather than passing them on to clients.[53]

If you do not plan to work in a large law firm, you will probably not have a large staff to support the technology needed for your computing and research needs, which makes the new technology requirements even more of a challenge for solos and small firms. However, considering that your options for legal research should include low-cost research services, such as Casemaker or Fastcase, having access to a quality legal research service should not be cost prohibitive. Additionally, flat-rate contracts with Bloomberg Law, Lexis Advance®, and Westlaw Edge are surprisingly affordable for

---

[50] Cass v. 1410088 Ontario Inc., 2018 ONSC 6959 (cited in Jennifer Wondracek, *Law Students—Avoid Malpractice and Embrace Technology!*, ABA FOR LAW STUDENTS: BEFORE THE BAR, (Feb. 20, 2019), https://abaforlawstudents.com/2019/02/20/law-students-avoid-malpractice-and-embrace-technology/.

[51] Id.

[52] *See* In Zynga Game Networks v. Ekran, 2010 WL 3463630 (N.D. Cal. August 31, 2010); American Small Business League v. U.S. Small Bus. Admin., 2005 WL 2206486 at *2 (N.D. Cal. September 12, 2005).

[53] *See* Rachel M. Zahorsky, Firms Wave Goodbye to Billing for Research Costs, ABA Journal, Nov. 14, 2012. http://www.abajournal.com/lawscribbler/article/firms_wave_goodbye_to_billing_for_research_costs.

solos and new practitioners.[54] The decisions you will need to make for legal research hinge on the balance of time and money, and which is most important to successfully represent your client.

The artificial intelligence and litigation analytics now incorporated into Bloomberg Law, Lexis Advance®, and Westlaw Edge may seem expensive, but are intended to save time, which will ultimately save your client money. When deciding how to balance these costs, consider that AI will most likely find what you need. . .can you? As CEO and co-founder of Fastcase, Ed Walters, said, ". . .as the quality of work product created by lawyers augmented with AI surpasses the work created without AI, it is clear that lawyers will soon have a professional responsibility to employ new techniques."[55]

Traditional fee structures based on the billable hour may need to be revised to include flat-rate options. If you spend enough time on any legal research project, you should eventually come to a full understanding of the issue. However, is the amount of time you spend on research, which is later billed back to your client, the most efficient use of your time and the most cost-effective use of your client's money? Both Lexis Advance® and Westlaw Edge offer transactional pricing, which allows attorneys to anticipate the cost of representation based on the amount of time they expect to spend on a given matter and the amount of information they will need to find to support their client. If a research service that employs AI can find what you need in a few seconds, can you justify spending hours of time doing research? "Any legal work that depends on collecting and analyzing historical data such as past judicial decisions, including legal opinions or evaluating likely litigation outcomes, will become the dominion of AI. No human lawyer stands a chance

---

[54]   Insert web sites with pricing.
[55]   Ed Walters, *The Model Rules of Autonomous Conduct: Ethical Responsibilities of Lawyers and Artificial Intelligence*, 35 GA. ST. UNIV. L. R. 1073, 1076 (2019).

against the formidable processing power of a mainframe when it comes to sifting through voluminous data."[56]

An example of a legal task that demonstrates the power of AI is a contract review. Employment contracts, non-disclosure agreements, or commercial loan agreements all contain standard, boilerplate language, but require an attorney's review for certain criteria, such as a choice of law provision. In 2017, J.P. Morgan Chase made headlines for using software that reviews contracts in seconds, instead of hours human lawyers would take for the same task.[57] "The bank says the software has helped reduce loan-servicing mistakes that were often attributable to human error in interpreting 12,000 new contracts per year."[58] Although AI can save time, attorneys need to understand the limits and risks associated with technology,[59] which brings us right back to a lawyer's duty of competence, or "the legal knowledge, skill, thoroughness and preparation reasonably necessary for the representation."[60] Artificial intelligence relies on correct data and has little or no way of determining whether errors are present in any particular data set without human help.

There is a law librarians' listserv[61] where law librarians across the country discuss everything related to legal research. With the

---

[56] Lauri Donahue, *A Primer on Using Artificial Intelligence in the Legal Profession*, HARVARD J. OF LAW AND TECHNOLOGY JOLT DIGEST (Jan. 3, 2018), https://jolt.law.harvard.edu/digest/a-primer-on-using-artificial-intelligence-in-the-legal-profession.

[57] Deborah Cassens Weiss, *JP Morgan Chase Uses Tech to Save 360,000 Hours of Annual Work by Lawyers and Loan Officers*, ABA J. (Mar. 2, 2017), http://www.abajournal.com/news/article/jpmorgan_chase_uses_tech_to_save_360000_hours_of_annual_work_by_lawyers_and.

[58] Id.

[59] MODEL RULES OF PROF'L CONDUCT r. 1.1 cmt. 8 (AM. BAR ASS'N 2018).

[60] Id.

[61] Lawlib is the law librarian's listserv hosted by U.C. Davis. Mary E. Matuszak, Director of Library Services at the New York County District Attorney's Office, finds and posts most of the errors. Ms. Matuszak compiled a spreadsheet of errors she had tracked since mid-October-December 2018 and there were more than 40 errors! Since that time, additional errors have been reported every day in 2019. Spreadsheet on file with author.

recent explosion of litigation analytic, an "error of the day" post has begun. Law librarians from academic, court, and law firm libraries are finding inaccuracies in the data made available through the analytics on Lexis Advance®, Westlaw Edge, and other legal research services. Once an error has been identified and shared with the listserv, the responsible research service will respond with how the error has likely occurred and an explanation of how the research service's engineers are working to resolve the error. It's a little alarming that new errors are found every day!

Some of these errors are bad links or typos, but some of the errors could taint the results of a data set derived from the search algorithms or artificial intelligence software.[62] As the saying goes, bad data in, bad data out.[63] Some of the errors reported on the law librarians' listserv include inaccurate dates, data linked to different judges or lawyers with the same or a similar name, or jurisdictions confused with similar abbreviations (is VA for Virginia or Veteran's Affairs?). Often the inaccuracies stem directly from the source inputting the information, such as court personnel. According to a LexisNexis® professional, when an attorney leaves one firm to join another, the next time that attorney enters their contact information into PACER, PACER retroactively assigns all former cases to the new law firm. When data is "dumped" into Lexis Advance®, the data is "cleansed" to "correct docket sheet information to ensure data accuracy."[64]

---

[62] Legal vendor representatives also subscribe to the law librarians' listserv and alert the powers-that-be within their organization of the inaccuracies. The vendor representatives will respond to the error post with an acknowledgement of the problem and when the error will be fixed. If you find errors in your research data, contact the publisher and report it.

[63] Eric Shrok, *Regulations Won't Kill AI—Bad Data Will*, FORBES (Sept. 4, 2018), https://www.forbes.com/sites/forbestechcouncil/2018/09/04/regulations-wont-kill-ai-bad-data-will/#57bcb2e63405.

[64] LexisNexis®, Analytics Comparison, https://www.google.com/url?sa=t&rct=j&q=&esrc=s&source=web&cd=1&ved=2ahUKEwi4p9vg86vlAhUCXawKHayeDZ8QFjAA egQIAhAC&url=https%3A%2F%2Fwww.lexisnexis.com%2FInfoPro%2Fliterature-reference%2Fm%2Fmediagallery%2F159%2Fdownload.aspx&usg=AOvVaw1v3C0n1-oPh MZDkst26OPx.

Humans and computers alike make mistakes. If you use information gleaned from AI, please consider it as you would any another legal research tool, such as Shepard's. When you Shepardize a court's opinion, all good attorneys know they need to read any negative treatment in the case before dismissing the opinion outright. Legal research services that employ AI software should be used in the same manner. The resulting product (contract) or data set (opinions decided by Judge X) should be reviewed for any inconsistencies or errors. This may involve using more than one source of information, or using a low cost legal research service and a legal research service that incorporates AI. This all relates to a lawyer's duty of competence, related to technology, now required of all lawyers.

CHAPTER 7

Research for Upper Level Writing

Over a decade ago, the American Bar Association amended the Standards of the Program of Legal Education to include more "writing experiences" with more rigor.[1] However, outside of the top tier of law schools, legal education primarily focuses on how to prepare professionals to practice law, and not how to engage in scholarly pursuits. When law professors engage in scholarly writing, it is as a subject law expert to explore an area of law more in-depth. Law professors engage in scholarly pursuits to stimulate their intellect and join their peers in discussions that far exceed the scope of a typical classroom discussion. Practitioners also engage in scholarly pursuits, as experts in their field of law. The law school rigorous writing standard places law students in the same arena as their professors and mentors, but long before they become experts in any subject area.

---

[1]   Standard 302 was amended in 2003 to include "at least one additional rigorous writing experience after the first year" with "substantial legal writing instruction." Standard 303 was revised again in 2017 to allow one course to meet either the upper level writing or simulation course requirements, but not both. *See* 2017-2018 STANDARD AND RULES OF PROCEDURE FOR APPROVAL OF LAW SCHOOLS, https://www.americanbar.org/groups/legal_education/resources/standards.html.

This creates quite a challenge for students. Unlike law professors or practitioners who write law review articles, law students must first develop a basis of understanding in their subject area and learn the doctrine. Next, they need to convert the practical legal writing skills they have learned in law school into skills suited for scholarly writing. Depending on the timing of when students need these credits, there will only be a few courses to choose from and the options may not be entirely within the students' preferred area of research. Once the student selects a course, then they need to select a topic, make certain it is unique, and quickly get up-to-speed on the issue to write an article with no fewer than 5,000 words in about 15 weeks.

Ready? Go!

The legal research skills developed during the first year of law school will help you to find resources help you become a better writer. Like any other legal research project, when you do not know where to begin, look for an expert on your subject area, or in this case, two. For your doctrinal subject, look for law professors who have written articles in your subject area. For upper level writing help, look for law professors who specialize in teaching law students how to write. Doctrinal professors are usually more interested in teaching legal doctrine, not legal writing, hence the need for more than one expert. Not surprisingly, law professors who teach legal writing often engage and explore methods on how best to teach law students how to write scholarly articles.

Begin your research in the law library. The following books are most likely in your law library's collection (this is not an exhaustive list—ask a reference librarian or a legal writing professor for additional suggestions):

- Elizabeth Fajans & Mary R. Falk's SCHOLARLY WRITING FOR LAW STUDENTS: SEMINAR PAPERS, LAW REVIEW NOTES AND LAW REVIEW COMPETITION PAPERS (5TH ED. 2017).

- Eugene Volokh, ACADEMIC LEGAL WRITING: LAW REVIEW ARTICLES, STUDENT NOTES, SEMINAR PAPERS, AND GETTING ON LAW REVIEW (5TH ED. 2016).

- Jessica L. Clark & Kristen E. Murray, SCHOLARLY WRITING: IDEAS, EXAMPLES, AND EXECUTION (2010).

- Wendy Laura Belcher, WRITING YOUR JOURNAL ARTICLE IN 12 WEEKS: A GUIDE TO ACADEMIC PUBLISHING SUCCESS (2009).

Additionally, there are several law review articles on how to write a law review article, available on Bloomberg Law, HeinOnline, Lexis Advance®, or Westlaw Edge:

- Richard Delgado, *How to Write a Law Review Article*, 20 U.S.F.L. REV. 445 (1986).

- Eugene Volokh, *Writing a Student Article*, 48 J. OF LEGAL EDUC. 247 (1998).

- Ruthann Robson, *Law Students as Legal Scholars: An Essay/Review of Scholarly Writing Law for Law Students and Academic Legal Writing*, 7 N.Y. CITY L. REV. 195 (2004).

- Claire R. Kelly, *An Evolutionary Endeavor: Teaching Scholarly Writing to Law Students*, 12 LEG. WRITING 285 (2006).

- Fred R. Shapiro & Michelle Pearse, *The Most-Cited Law Review Articles of All Time*, 110 MICH. L. REV. 1483 (2012).

1. Finding a Topic

Practitioners, judges, and academics read law review articles for a variety of purposes, but often to deepen their level of understanding about a legal issue or subject matter or learn how an area of law has evolved over time. Legal scholars have time to devote to exploring legal issues in depth through study and discussions with their peers, and this results in providing a very valuable service to legal practitioners who are usually pressed for time. Law reviews also provide a forum for exploring legal issues that develop outside of the courtroom.[2] Law review articles are also a great resource to use as a starting point for researching any area of law.

When you begin to research an area of law, you will also learn which issues already have numerous law review articles on the subject and do not need another law student's examination. Your first job is to find an issue that is unique or novel. If you are trying to find a topic, begin with your textbook. Some textbooks offer Notes and/or Questions at the end of a chapter to help stimulate class discussion. These Notes and/or Questions might also form the basis of a law review article. The Notes and/or Questions often point out circuit splits, where two U.S. Circuit Courts of Appeal have examined the same legal issue, but come to a different conclusion. When you find a legal issue where reasonable minds can disagree, you have also found an issue for an upper level writing paper.

Bloomberg Law[3] has curated a lot of great resources for students on law review which can also be used by students writing upper level papers. Log in to Bloomberg Law and follow the link to

---

[2]   Melvin A. Eisenberg, *Corporate Law and Social Norms*, 99 COLUM. L. REV. 1253, 1254 (1999).

[3]   Look for *Law Review Resources* on Bloomberg Law, in the *Law School Success* box.

Law Review Resources in the **Law School Success** box. The **Find a Topic** box helps explain what your upper level paper will look like:

> A note or comment is a scholarly paper that discusses a relevant legal issue and is generally 20 to 30 pages long. Your goal in writing a note or comment is to provide a unique perspective on an issue of law, take a position on an emerging legal issue, or offer a new interpretation of an existing rule of law.[4]

a. *Circuit Splits*

I have two generic suggestions for students looking for upper level paper topics: circuit splits and 50-state statute surveys. Circuit splits are when two (or more) U.S. Circuit Courts of Appeal have decided the same legal issue, but have not come to the same conclusion. Circuit splits are perfect fodder for an upper level writing paper. Not only do you have at least two appellate courts that disagree on the same legal issue, but both courts have analyzed the legal issue and laid the groundwork for comparison. Besides, if the U.S. Supreme Court decides to review the decisions, they might just read your law review article! You can easily find circuit splits in the *United States Law Week*, which provides an updated Circuit Splits Chart every month. The chart is organized alphabetically by topic and analyzed by *U.S. Law Week* editors. Follow the link to the **Circuit Splits Chart** to review the current month's circuit splits, or add additional search terms to the **Circuit Splits Court Opinion Search**, and then narrow by court, judge, state, or topic.[5]

---

[4] Law Reviews and Journal, *Find a Topic*, https://www.bloomberglaw.com/page/law_reviews_and_journals.

[5] Reprinted with permission by Bloomberg Law. Copyright 2019.

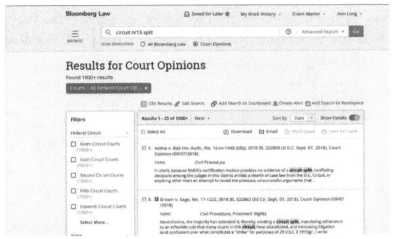

Reprinted from Bloomberg Law with permission. Copyright 2019,
The Bureau of National Affairs, Inc. All rights reserved.

Once you have identified a circuit split you are interested in, read the two cases. The courts may have applied a different rule to reach their decisions, or applied same rule, but came to a different conclusion. Regardless, both cases will provide you with additional cases that support each court's conclusion. Read all of the underlying case law and then suggest which court found the "best" solution, based on your understanding of the issue.[6] Support your argument by looking for U.S. District Court cases outside of the Circuit Courts you are comparing that agree (or disagree) with your thesis.

b. 50-State Surveys and State Subject Compilations

My second suggestion for students looking for an upper level paper topic is to compare different states' laws. There is a terrific resource for this type of research, available in print in any academic

---

[6]   To find examples of law review articles that have discussed circuit splits, search for circuit splits in the title of the article and sort by most cited. Westlaw Edge example: ti("circuit splits"). Lexis Advance® example: title("circuit splits").

law library, on HeinOnline, or Westlaw: the NATIONAL SURVEY OF STATE LAWS.[7] Recently, a student asked for my help in finding an issue within the broad topic of domestic violence. The NATIONAL SURVEY OF STATE LAWS is organized alphabetically by broad topic.[8] The domestic violence statute comparison chart has several narrower issues, including mandatory or discretionary arrest laws. The chart clearly shows which states require a mandatory arrest, or whether the officer has any discretion. If you are using this resource on HeinOnline, you can check a box next to those states you would like to compare, if you are only interested in a select number of states or a particular region. Once you have the list of codified statutes, then you can find related state case law that has interpreted those statutes for further comparison.[9]

---

[7] Richard Lieter, NATIONAL SURVEY OF STATE LAWS (8th ed. 2019). Also available in print in most academic law libraries. The 7th edition is available on Westlaw.

[8] Under the broad topic of Family Laws are charts comparing state statutes on abortion, adoption, annulment and prohibited marriage, child abuse, child custody, child support guidelines, domestic violence, grounds for divorce, marital property, marriage age requirements, and protective orders.

[9] Using Bloomberg Law, Lexis Advance®, or Westlaw Edge, find the state statutory section listed in the state survey chart, then look for case law references in the annotations. If you like this idea, take a look at the format of the winning article from the American Constitution Society's Constance Baker Motley National Student Writing Competition written by Hana M. Sahdev, *Juvenile Miranda Waivers and Wrongful Convictions*, 20 U. PA. J. CONST. L. 1212 (2018).

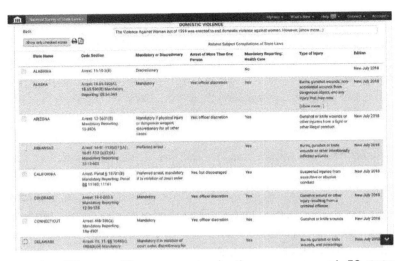

Be diligent with your research—there are several 50-state surveys available on Westlaw Edge and Lexis Advance®. Begin typing "50 state survey" into the general search box on either research service and autofill will provide links to additional resources.

Another nifty option for finding (and creating) statutory surveys is on Bloomberg Law. From the **Law School Success** box, follow the link to **State Law Chart Builders**[10] (under the Practice Tools section).[11] Although the state survey options on Bloomberg Law are not as comprehensive as the NATIONAL SURVEY OF STATE LAWS, you may find a topic of interest. The broad topics available are Banking and Consumer Finance, Blue Sky Securities, Corporate, Environmental, Health Care, Labor and Employment, and Privacy and Data Security, and Tax.[12]

---

[10]   Reprinted with permission by Bloomberg Law. Copyright 2019.

[11]   BLOOMBERG   LAW,   https://www.bloomberglaw.com/page/chart_builders_home.

[12]   Id.

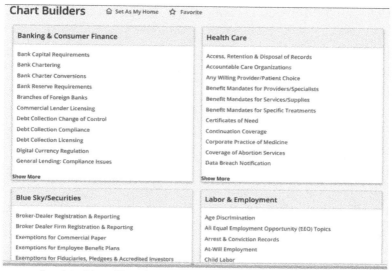

Reprinted from Bloomberg Law with permission. Copyright 2019,
The Bureau of National Affairs, Inc. All rights reserved.

There are numerous issues within each broad topic to help you narrow your focus, and once you have selected an issue, you can further narrow to the specific statutory provision you are interested in. Once you have selected an issue, you can select specific states or statutory provisions to compare. For example, under the broad topic of Privacy & Data Security, you may be interested in comparing state statutes on the notification requirements of organizations in the event of a data breach.[13] The chart builder allows you to select by jurisdiction and topic.[14]

---

[13] The Privacy Rights Clearinghouse keeps track of data breaches at their site, https://privacyrights.org/data-breaches. You can search by breach type, organization type, and/or type of organization.

[14] *Bloomberg Law State Chart Builder: State Data Breach Notification Requirements*, https://www.bloomberglaw.com/bbna/chart/43/404. Reprinted with permission by Bloomberg Law. Copyright 2019.

Reprinted from Bloomberg Law with permission. Copyright 2019,
The Bureau of National Affairs, Inc. All rights reserved.

In the event you cannot find a 50-state survey on your issue, make sure your preemption check includes all available 50-state surveys, related treatises, and law review articles. Subject treatises will often include a 50-state statutory survey in an appendix and many law review authors will create a 50-state survey to support their position. If you are looking for a survey that was created as the focus of discussion in a law review article, use the Lexis Advance® footnote field search.[15] You can search for your issue in either the title or summary fields, and then narrow your results to those law review articles that include state surveys cited within their footnotes. Alternatively, you can search the footnote field for state surveys and narrow your results to jurisdiction or practice area/topic on Lexis Advance®.

---

[15] Lexis Advance® is the only legal research service that offers footnotes as a field search option.

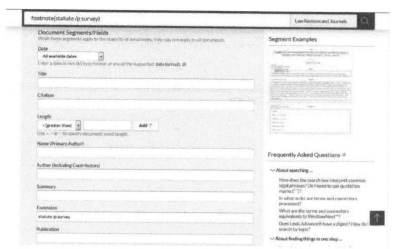

Reprinted from LexisNexis® with permission. Copyright 2019 LexisNexis®.
All rights reserved.

If you have a subject area in mind, but cannot find a 50-state survey on point with your issue, look in HeinOnline's Subject Compilations of State laws, which provides

> access to more than 26,000 bibliographic records from Cheryl Nyberg's Subject Compilations Bibliography Series. Many records contain extensive annotations with links directly to articles and other documents residing in HeinOnline. In addition to a searchable database, HeinOnline also includes the exact replicas of the original bound volumes.[16]

HeinOnline also provides LibGuides to help explain the content in each database and provide general search tips. "Cheryl Nyberg's *Subject Compilations of State Laws* has long been recognized as the most comprehensive source for identifying thousands of articles, books, government documents, looseleaf services, court opinions and Internet sites that compare state laws on hundreds of

---

[16] From the HeinOnline Subject Compilations of State Law scope note.

subjects."[17] Also helpful is an alphabetical list of subjects, that may be helpful in leading you to a subject you might be interested in learning more about.

c. *Symposiums*

If my top two suggestions do not appeal to you, try looking for topics legal scholars in your subject area are currently discussing. Look for law review symposium issues dedicated to your area of interest. Symposiums are usually single-day conferences where legal scholars and experts meet with similar minded folks to share their ideas and engage in discussions on recent developments in their areas of expertise. In addition, many law schools host symposiums on current and/or local topics of interest, so if your law school has a symposium scheduled in the near future, you may have a front-row seat to listen to legal experts present their research.

To find symposiums on your topic, begin your search by selecting a law reviews and journals database on Bloomberg Law, HeinOnline, Lexis Advance®, or Westlaw Edge. Now search for

---

[17] From the HeinOnline Subject Compilation of State Laws LibGuide, https://lib guides-heinonline-org.lmunet.idm.oclc.org/subject-compilations-of-state-laws.

articles that include the word "symposium" and your broad subject area in the title field. Next, sort your results by date to see the most current symposium topics. As you can see in the results that follow, there are a plethora of symposiums on the broad subject area of law and technology.

Lexis Advance® advanced search example: title(symposium AND (technology /s law))

- SYMPOSIUM—GOVERNANCE OF EMERGING TECHNOLOGIES: LAW, POLICY, AND ETHICS

- ALBANY LAW JOURNAL OF SCIENCE AND TECHNOLOGY'S SYMPOSIUM

- TEN CHALLENGES IN TECHNOLOGY AND INTELLECTUAL PROPERTY LAW FOR 2015: REMARKS AT THE WAKE FOREST JOURNAL OF BUSINESS AND INTELLECTUAL PROPERTY LAW SYMPOSIUM

- INTRODUCTION TO THE SYMPOSIUM EDITION: NEW TECHNOLOGY AND OLD LAW: RETHINKING NATIONAL SECURITY

- SYMPOSIUM: DISRUPTIVE INNOVATION IN LAW AND TECHNOLOGY

After you have compiled a list of current symposium subjects, you can begin to narrow to find a more specific issue—policy and ethics, intellectual property, national security, or disruptive innovation. Pay attention to the law review hosting the symposium and revise your search to include that law review and symposium topic. You may also want to visit the hosting law review's website to see if this symposium topic is an annual event. Additionally, it may be easier to read all of a symposium issue from the hosting law review's website, and usually law school publications are available for free.

The American Association of Law Schools (AALS) provides a list of upcoming symposia hosted at member law schools.[18] Although it is up to each individual member law school to submit their symposia to AALS for inclusion on this list, this may be the most comprehensive source for finding symposiums on your topic. The list of symposia usually include a link to the symposium's announcement, which will also include links to past symposia on your topic.

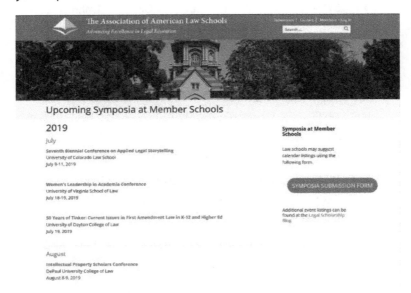

d. *Legal Trends*

Bloomberg Law also offers **In Focus Resources**, which provide the "latest news, commentary, litigation filings, regulatory developments, and practice tools on emerging issues and other topics of note to legal practitioners."[19] There are dozens of topics

---

[18] AMERICAN ASSOCIATION OF LAW SCHOOLS, https://www.aals.org/home/upcoming-symposia-member-schools/?utm_source=email&utm_medium=informz&utm_campaign=AALS.

[19] From the Bloomberg Law *In Focus Resources* topics note, https://www.bloomberglaw.com/page/infocus_home.

covered, some that may be of interest include Autonomous Vehicles, Blockchain Technology, GDPR Compliance, Immigration Issues for Employers, Initial Coin Offerings, Medical Marijuana, Opioid Litigation, Sexual Harassment, and Transgender Issues in the Workplace. There are also archived **In Focus** pages, in the event you are interested in writing about a topic that is no longer current. For example, one archive is "The Trump Administration: First 100 Days." The archived **In Focus** collections are organized under three broad topics, which include Banking & Finance, Intellectual Property, and Law & Politics.[20]

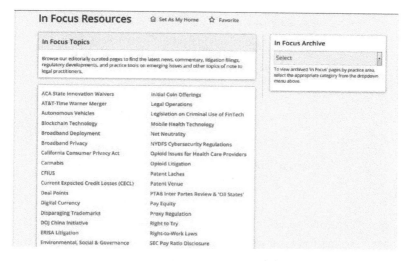

If the options above have not lead you to something interesting to write about, visit an association's website. Associations are groups of people who are usually working toward a common goal or purpose and their websites usually have current topics of interest of that association. There are more than 24,000 national, regional, state, and local associations.[21] If you are enrolled in a cross-disciplinary upper-level writing course, such as Education Law, you

---

[20] Reprinted with permission by Bloomberg Law. Copyright 2019.

[21] ENCYCLOPEDIA OF ASSOCIATIONS (57th ed. 2018). The encyclopedia is also available through Gale database subscriptions.

may be interested in visiting a related association's website to get an idea of what that association is currently interested in. Association websites usually end with .org (organization). The following example is telling Google to return only those websites that end in .org, to avoid any commercial websites.[22]

Google example: **org: education association**

In addition to learning what is of interest to members of any given association, you might also be interested in what issues the general public is interested in, or what the general public is Googling most often. **Google Trends** is a search engine designed just for this purpose. Search for your topic (below is the search results for education) and find out how a particular topic's interest has changed over time, which regions or states are the most interested in your topic, and related topics or queries. The regions or states that appear as the most interested may help you identify which state statutes to begin your research and/or compare. For example,

---

[22] Google also considers geolocation when search results are displayed, which is why the Tennessee Education Association appears toward the top of my results list.

if you are interested in writing a paper on how state income tax affects public education, you can easily identify the seven states that do not collect state income tax.[23] Additionally, if you are researching newer trends or trying to find out which states are actively discussing various subtopics of education, such as magnet schools, a Google Trends search may help.

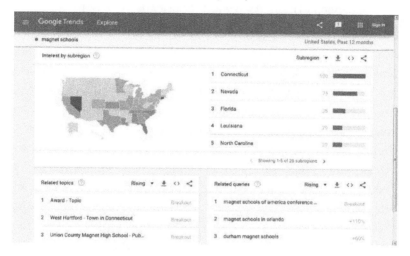

Looking at the search results above, it appears Connecticut, Nevada, and Florida may have recently passed education laws or have introduced legislation regarding magnet schools. Additionally, the related queries of "Magnet Schools in Orlando" and "Durham Magnet Schools" might suggest that Florida and North Carolina are two good states to begin your research on statutes.

Another excellent free resource for researching legal trends and how legal issues have developed over time are Congressional Research Service Reports.

The Congressional Research Service (CRS) works exclusively for the United States Congress, providing

---

[23] Dan Dzombak (The Motley Fool), *These States Have No Income Tax*, USA TODAY (Apr. 26, 2014), https://www.usatoday.com/story/money/personalfinance/2014/04/26/these-states-have-no-income-tax/8116161/.

policy and legal analysis to committees and Members of both the House and Senate, regardless of party affiliation. As a legislative branch agency within the Library of Congress, CRS has been a valued and respected resource on Capitol Hill for more than a century. CRS is well-known for analysis that is authoritative, confidential, objective and nonpartisan. Its highest priority is to ensure that Congress has 24/7 access to the nation's best thinking.[24]

There are five areas of research that the CRS focuses on: American Law; Domestic Social Policy; Foreign Affairs, Defense and Trade; Government and Finance; Resources, Science and Industry. Every year the CRS produces hundreds of new reports, based on the current federal legislative issues. Although the CRS works exclusively for the U.S. Congress, the reports and memoranda they compile are available to the general public.[25] A general search for "education" returns 232 reports, including primers or overviews of federal Acts, reports on issues related to education (such as accreditation, financial aid, and college savings plans), and the history or status of specific legislative attempts. CRS reports will summarize the topic and discuss the major issues Congress needs to consider while drafting new legislation. If nothing else, CRS reports may help you narrow a broad topic, such as education, or introduce you to a more current issue that has not been written about.

---

[24] CONGRESSIONAL RESEARCH SERVICE, https://crsreports.congress.gov/. Another resource, CQ Researcher, provides in-depth, single-themed, 12,000-word reports on health, social trends, criminal justice, international affairs, education, the environment, technology, and the economy. Each report contains an introductory overview; background and chronology on the topic; an assessment of the current situation; tables and maps; pro/con statements from representatives of opposing positions; and bibliographies of key sources. CQ Researcher contains archives of all CQ Researcher reports from 1991, to present and all Editorial Research Reports from 1923 to 1991. CQ Researcher requires a subscription. Please check with your law library for access.

[25] There is a searchable database of CRS Reports at https://crsreports.congress.gov/.

e. *ProQuest Thesis and Dissertations*

ProQuest publishes several thesis and dissertation collections, but the Humanities and Social Sciences collection is a subscription held by most academic law libraries. If you are interested in a cross-disciplinary topic, such as criminal justice or business intelligence, it is possible a doctoral student may have published research for their PhD that will be helpful for your paper. From the ProQuest Thesis and Dissertations database description for the Humanities and Social Sciences collection. . .

. . . the world's most comprehensive collection of dissertations and theses. The official digital dissertations archive for the Library of Congress and the database of record for graduate research. PQDT—Full Text includes millions of searchable citations to dissertation and theses from around the world from 1861 to the present day together with over a million full text dissertations that are available for download in PDF format. Over 2.1 million titles are available for purchase as printed copies. The database offers full text for most of the dissertations added since 1997 and strong retrospective full text coverage for older graduate works.

More than 70,000 new full text dissertations and theses are added to the database each year through dissertations publishing partnerships with 700 leading academic institutions worldwide and collaborative retrospective digitization of dissertations through UMI's Digital Archiving and Access Program. Full Text dissertations are archived as submitted by the degree-granting institution. Some will be native PDF, some PDF image.

Each dissertation published since July 1980 includes a 350-word abstract written by the author. Master's theses published since 1988 include 150-word abstracts. Simple bibliographic citations are available for dissertations dating from 1637. Where available, PQDT— Full Text provides 24-page previews of dissertations and theses.[26]

2. Get Pocket, Get Organized, and Create an Outline

Before you go much further with your research, organize what you find by creating an account and installing the Get Pocket browser extension.[27] The Pocket button will appear on your browser's toolbar and when you find an article, an ebook, or a website on point with your research, click on the Pocket icon to save what you have found. Add metadata[28] tags to organize your research. Add additional metadata tags if the article might fit into more than one category. Which brings us to creating an outline. . .

If you are enrolled in an upper level writing class, you probably already know the broad subject area. To narrow your focus to an issue you would like to learn more about, open your textbook and glance through the Summary of Contents. This gives you a broad overview of your subject area. Your textbook is divided into either parts and chapters or chapters and subheadings. Within each chapter/subheading are the major cases and issues you will learn about over the next semester. Browse through the table of contents and consider some of the chapters/subheadings that you find the most interesting. Just as the table of contents is an outline for your

---

[26] From the ProQuest Dissertation and Thesis Global: Humanities and Social Sciences Collection scope note.

[27] Go to https://getpocket.com/ and sign up for free.

[28] Roughly translated, "metadata" is information about data. Or data about data. Or metadata.

book, you need to create an outline for the article you plan to research and discuss.

Many law review articles begin with a backstory, or the history or evolution of an issue. If you have not taken the time to read one of the law review articles on how to write a law review mentioned earlier, now would be a good time. The first article mentioned above, *How to Write a Law Review Article*,[29] begins by providing an outline. The second item on Delgado's outline is: What Varieties of Law Review Articles Are There?[30] Your outline will largely depend on the type of law review article you plan to write. Outlines help the reader know what to expect and help the writer stay focused and organized. As you begin your research, start creating metadata tags to describe each of the articles you find. Later, these metadata tags can help you develop your outline and show you where you need additional content.

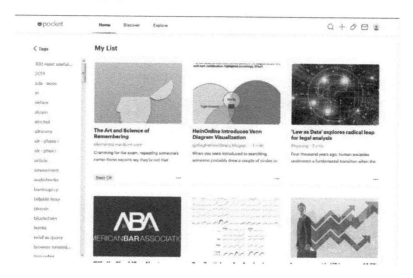

---

[29] Richard Delgado, *How to Write a Law Review Article*, 20 U.S.F.L. Rev. 445 (1986).

[30] Id. at 445.

Here is a snapshot of my Pocket home page and a sample of metadata tags I have created (on the left). Over time, you may find that some of your metadata tags have a lot of content and other tags need more content. Although Bloomberg Law, Lexis Advance®, and Westlaw Edge all offer folders for saving your research, the folders are not transferable from one service to the next. Pocket helps you to organize content from all sources you access using the internet in one tidy place, which will help you keep track of the resources you have consulted (also extremely helpful when you are adding your citations!).

In addition to internet resources, another resource is in your textbook: the Table of Contents. Once you have identified a chapter or subheading you are interested in, look for the leading cases discussed in your textbook. The major cases may lead you to some interesting articles and help you identify an issue you might like to write about. Use the party names of an interesting case to search for related law reviews and journals.

Westlaw Edge example: Secondary Sources,
Law Reviews & Journals

Advanced search: (woolley /s hoffmann-la roche)[31]

Results sorted by the Most Cited articles

---

[31] On my bookshelf, I happen to have SAMUEL ESTREICHER, MICHAEL C. HARPER & ELIZABETH C. TIPPETT'S, CASES AND MATERIALS ON EMPLOYMENT DISCRIMINATION AND EMPLOYMENT LAW THE FIELD AS PRACTICED (5th ed. 2016). The New Jersey Supreme Court case, *Woolley v. Hoffmann-La Roche, Inc.*, 491 A.2d 1257 (N.J. 1985) discusses at-will employment, employment contracts, and wrongful dismissal and is cited in more than 160 law review articles!

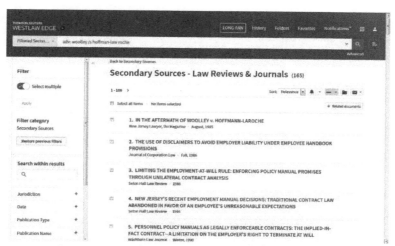

Reprinted from Westlaw with permission. Copyright 2019,
Thomson Reuters. All rights reserved.

In law school, you have access to several research services—
use all of them! Although all of the major legal research services
have a law reviews and journals database, the coverage, content,
and search options will vary by service. HeinOnline has the most in-
depth coverage, starting with the very first issues of all law reviews,
but can be tricky to search.[32] The coverage for law reviews and
journals varies by title on Lexis Advance® and Westlaw, but
generally begins in the mid-1990s. If you are looking for law review
articles that discuss older cases, such as the *Woolley* case, decided
in 1985, you should begin your research with HeinOnline. Running
our same search in the HeinOnline Law Journal Library database
results in more than 400 results and gives us another sorting option:
by Most-Cited Author.

---

[32] The HeinOnline Law Journal Library provides access to a collection of over
2,600 legal periodicals. "Coverage for all journals is from inception and goes through
the most currently published issues allowed based on contracts with publishers. About
90% of journals are available through the current issue or volume." (Quote taken from
the HeinOnline Law Journal Library description note.) The content is created from
original law review print journals that have been scanned using Optical Character
Resolution (OCR) software and saved as searchable PDFs (portable document format).

Unlike law professors who typically teach and write in specific subject areas and are well versed in their area of expertise, as a law student, you need to play catch-up fast. Your law professor will either know of the leading authors in their field, or know them personally through the conferences they attend. The Most-Cited Author sorting option helps law students learn which authors are considered to be the experts in their field, without having to invest in time spent attending conferences and eating rubber-chicken dinners. Now that you have a general idea of the Most Cited Authors, you can search for additional articles written by those authors to help expand your search.[33] Keep in mind your professor will know the leading authors in their field. If you do not read and cite to the articles written by the leading authors, your professor will not believe that your research is thorough.

While HeinOnline will provide you with the most in-depth coverage, another database, SSRN (Social Science Research

---

[33] You may also consider searching for law review articles written by your professor or the author of your textbook. Ask your professor to suggest well-known authors in your area of research.

Network),[34] provides you with the most breadth. SSRN offers research networks where scholars can submit their research and invite other scholars to download and comment on their work or learn about upcoming conferences and meetings. The Legal Scholarship Network (LSN) is where you will find most legal scholars writing about legal topics, but SSRN is home to all academic disciplines, which makes it a good place to search for cross-disciplinary research topics. Within the Legal Scholarship Network (LSN) is a list of LSN Subject Matter Journals. Expand this section to view an alphabetical list of journals in your subject area. Here is a screenshot of criminal law and procedure and employment/labor journals.

---

[34] SSRN requires membership for access. Go to https://www.ssrn.com/en/ and check with your law library to find out if your law school has a subscription available for students. If not, you can request a free trial subscription, which may be enough for you to conduct the initial research you need to find an article topic.

⊟ **Criminal Law & Procedure eJournals** ① 25,196 Papers
     Corrections & Sentencing Law & Policy eJournal ① 4,281 Papers
     Criminal Law & Procedure eJournal, Archives of 1996-2006 ① 2,333 Papers
     Criminal Law eJournal ① 5,983 Papers
     Criminal Procedure eJournal ① 6,520 Papers
     Criminology eJournal ① 4,157 Papers
     International, Transnational & Comparative Criminal Law eJournal ① 6,191 Papers
     White Collar Crime eJournal ① 1,733 Papers
     Cybersecurity, Data Privacy & eDiscovery Law & Policy eJournal ① 1,629 Papers
     Cyberspace Law - Student Authors eJournal ① 689 Papers
     Cyberspace Law eJournal ① 8,597 Papers
     Democratization: Building States & Democratic Processes eJournal ① 2,436 Papers
     Disability Law eJournal ① 2,031 Papers
     Discrimination, Law & Justice eJournal ① 12,381 Papers
     Economic Inequality & the Law eJournal ① 4,154 Papers
⊟ Education Law eJournal ① 2,943 Papers
     LSN: Education Law: College & Graduate Education (Topic) ① 1,343 Papers
     LSN: Education Law: Primary & Secondary Education (Topic) ① 1,633 Papers
     Elder Law Studies eJournal ① 1,250 Papers
⊟ **Employment, Labor, Compensation & Pension Law eJournals** ① 13,100 Papers
     ⊟ Economic Perspectives on Employment & Labor Law eJournal ① 2,811 Papers
         LSN: Empirical Studies of Employment & Labor Law (Topic) ① 1,508 Papers
         LSN: Theoretical Perspectives on Employment & Labor Law (Topic) ① 1,300 Papers
     ⊟ Employee Benefits, Compensation & Pension Law eJournal ① 5,310 Papers
         LSN: Compensation Law (Topic) ① 652 Papers
         LSN: Employee Benefits Law (Topic) ① 1,332 Papers
         LSN: Pension Law (Topic) ① 1,334 Papers
     Employment & Labor Law Abstracts eJournal, Archives of Vols. 2-7, 2001-06 ① 1,057 Papers
     ⊟ Employment Law eJournal ① 4,083 Papers
         LSN: Employment Contract Law (Topic) ① 896 Papers
         LSN: Employment Statutes (Topic) ① 2,176 Papers
         LSN: Employment Tort Law (Topic) ① 544 Papers
     Employment, Labor, Compensation & Pension Law eJournal, Archives of 1997-2000 ① 714 Papers
     ⊟ International Employment & Labor Law eJournal ① 1,560 Papers

After you have identified a journal that focuses on your subject area of interest, you can follow the link to that journal to read related articles on point with your issue. You can sort by download to view the articles that have been downloaded the most often,[35] by date, or by title. There is also an option to search within a journal or run an advanced search for your keywords in the title; title and abstract; or title, abstract, and full text; however, these options search *all* of SSRN, not just the journal you have selected. Use the

---

[35] Everyone wants to be popular and lawyers are no exception. Legal scholars want their research to be of value to their peers and to the legal profession as a whole. Pay attention to the number of downloads an article has received. If an article discussing your issue has a high number of downloads, it is likely that your professor will have read the article and expect you to cite it in your article. Extensive citation demonstrates that your research is thorough. Alternatively, if an article has a high number of downloads and you miss it, your topic might not be novel or unique.

sorting options to view the articles published in the journal you have
selected.

At this point, you have probably identified a number of articles
of interest and saved them all to Pocket. Now is the time to start
reading the articles you have found. While you are reading the
articles, pay attention to a couple of things, namely, how the
articles are organized. Most of the longer law review articles will
have an outline at the beginning of the article. Read the outline to
identify the section(s) you are most interested in. Use the article's
outline just as would you use headnotes in an opinion to help you
focus on a particular legal issue. You may need to add additional
metadata tags to help develop your own outline, if your initial tags
were too broad. After you have read a number of articles, you may
want to move some of them to a folder that is related, but not
exactly on point with your issue. Resist the temptation to delete
these articles from Pocket—they may provide you with a counter-

argument that is still under development. As you continue to read the articles you have collected and tagged, you will learn more about your issue. This will spawn more research ideas, more tagging, and more reading. Continue this process until you are satisfied with your issue and have a fairly solid outline.

3. Preemption Search Strategies to Make Certain Your Claim Is Unique

Now that you have an outline, do one more search. Search Lexis Advance® and Westlaw for law reviews and journals using the exact issues you have decided to write about. Let's say you have decided to write an article comparing states' slayer statutes and whether these laws apply to victims of domestic violence who have killed their spouses. You will quickly find several articles that have discussed this issue. Now your job is to read these articles, figure out which issues the authors have thoroughly discussed, and decide whether you have anything additional to add. It is possible you disagree with the chorus of authors, or the published authors have overlooked a related issue. A preemption search will help you become very familiar with your issue, the authors publishing in your subject area, and help you focus your research on issues that are unique. Make certain you cite to these authors in your own article to give you credibility with your professor and anyone else who reads your article.[36]

---

[36] This is no different that citing case law. When you are writing a brief in support of a legal issue, you want your reader to see that you have researched the issue thoroughly and that all of the cited cases in your jurisdiction support your argument. Similar to court hierarchies, where you always want to cite to the court of last resort in any given jurisdiction, law reviews are ranked, just like law schools are ranked. A University of Oregon professor, Bryce Clayton Newell, has created a meta ranking of law reviews based on three popular law review ranking indexes. Prof. Newell's version provides a ranking of the "top flagship law reviews at US law schools." https://blogs.uoregon.edu/bcnewell/meta-ranking/. It averages three indexes for 192 law reviews, with available rankings from the US News report (law school peer reputation and overall rankings averaged from 2011-2020), the Washington & Lee law review rankings (2010-2017), and Google Scholar (July 2019 only).

If you find that your issue has been discussed widely,[37] consider narrowing your topic to a specific jurisdiction or sub-issue. We can narrow the issue above (slayer statutes and domestic violence) with the *Search Within Results* using the keywords: Tennessee or (elder! or retire!). Now you have the original set of articles that discuss your issue broadly, and results that focus on either the jurisdiction of Tennessee, on the two narrower issues, or possibly nothing at all. If your *Search Within Results* eliminates all of the articles, you've sufficiently narrowed down your topic to either a jurisdiction or an issue that is unique.

If you find that your issue has been discussed almost exactly as you had envisioned, you may need to broaden your topic. Consider providing a legislative history of the issue, or compare your state's statute with another state, or compare how various regions of the country have treated the issue. Use the same search strategies outlined above to identify additional jurisdictions that have similar statutes, or consider jurisdictions with completely different statutory approaches.[38] Either way, you can now begin researching case law within those jurisdictions to provide you with more fodder for discussion. As always, save all of the new research results to Pocket and organize by metadata tags. The Pocket icon will change color from red to black when you have already saved an article; however, one article or opinion can discuss several issues related to your topic and may be worth saving under more than one metadata tag.

Additionally, if the article you had hoped to write has already been written, if it was published several years ago, you could use that article as a starting point for an updated article that discusses current cases, statutory changes, or cultural shifts. You need to cite

---

[37] Searching "slayer statutes" and "domestic violence" returns 26 law review articles on Lexis Advance® and 30 on Westlaw Edge.

[38] The NATIONAL SURVEY FOR STATE LAWS would come in handy to help identify other states' statutes, supra note 6.

to the original author and make certain that what you write is not only new law, but from your own perspective.

At this point, you should have an outline and begin to feel confident that your issue is novel and unique. However, now is a good time to use all of the research services you have available to you to make certain that your article will add something new to the scholarly debate. If you have used Bloomberg Law, Lexis Advance®, and Westlaw for your research, turn to an index, such as the *Index to Legal Periodicals*[39] or the *Current Index to Legal Periodicals* (CILP). Your law library may have a separate subscription to both of these indexes, or you can search the Current Index to Legal Periodicals on Westlaw[40] or HeinOnline.[41] After this last step, you should have read enough law review articles to verify that your idea is unique. You have also researched the related statutes, regulations, and case law to provide you with the background necessary to competently discuss your issue. Now all you need is your professor's approval of your topic!

---

[39]   The *Index to Legal Periodicals & Books Full Text* is published by H.W. Wilson and available through EBSCOHost. From the scope note on EBSCOHost, *"Index to Legal Periodicals and Books Full Text* is an excellent resource for attorneys, educators, business people, law librarians, students, paralegal and others involved with the law, providing complete coverage of the most important English language legal information, with international coverage of scholarly articles, symposia, jurisdictional surveys, court decisions, legislation, books, book reviews and more. Full text is available for over 400 periodicals, many of them peer-reviewed, as far back as 1994."

[40]   From the scope note on Westlaw, "Weekly editions of the Current Index to Legal Periodicals, which indexes articles from more than 300 legal publications." The CILP.

[41]   The scope note on HeinOnline provides a bit more information, giving credit to the University of Washington Marian Gould Gallaher Law Library staff for "[p]roviding legal researchers with the fastest, most cost-effective current awareness tool is the goal of the law librarians and staff of the Marian Gould Gallagher Law Library. They have been preparing this not-for-profit publication weekly since 1948." As you might expect, HeinOnline provides the most depth in coverage for CILP, beginning in 1936–current.

4. Avoid Plagiarizing!

One of the unwritten job duties of a law professor is to read and remain current in their area of expertise. In fact, most of your law professors consider this task enjoyable. Consider this is as one of the reasons you cite all of the author's articles you use—if you somehow forget to do this, your professor may recognize the language from an article he or she has recently read. For the same reasons you cite to a plethora of case citations to support an argument in a legal memorandum, you want to cite to a plethora of law review authors, statutes, and case law to demonstrate you have done your due diligence in researching the legal issues thoroughly. The other reason to always cite to the original authority is to make certain that you DO NOT PLAGIARIZE.

Law professors have access to a plagiarism tool called Turnitin[42] (turn it in) that is used to compare the words in your article to words that appear in published articles. It's quick, it's easy, and it identifies all sorts of commonly used legal phrases and popular sayings, in addition to any phrases that appear to be verbatim or closely resembles the language from another source. According to Turnitin, there are ten types of plagiarism, ranging from a student's "cloning" of a section or portion of a published work to a "re-tweet" where the language has been properly cited, "but relies too closely on the text's original wording and/or structure."[43] Law professors take plagiarism seriously and law students should too. Plagiarism is considered a violation of a law school's honor code and if you are suspected of plagiarism, you may never get the opportunity to graduate from law school.

---

[42] For more information about plagiarism and the software that helps detect it, go to https://www.turnitin.com/divisions/higher-education.

[43] Become familiar with all ten to make certain you don't plagiarize! https://www.turnitin.com/static/plagiarism-spectrum/?_ga=2.237720130.311194 866.1537831831-946558907.1537831831.

Even if your law professor does not use Turnitin, or another type of software to detect plagiarism, they will probably recognize when you are using someone else's language and failed to properly reference it. When you borrow language or phrases from another person, your writing style changes. Your sentences will appear either more formal or more verbose than the rest of your paper and the plagiarized portion of your paper will stick out like a sore thumb.[44] If a reasonable person[45] is unsure of whether to include a reference to a common legal phrase or well-known saying, refer to your law school's plagiarism policies or ask your law professor. The best practice is to cite to everything you reference, including common legal phrases. You can find the origin of a legal phrase in a number of places; here are a few suggestions.

You could begin with a legal dictionary such as Black's[46] or Ballantine's[47] to find the origin of a legal phrase. You might also use a legal encyclopedia such as Corpus Juris Secundum (C.J.S.) or American Jurisprudence (Am. Jur. 2d). However, for common legal phrases, the best option might be to search a case law database on Westlaw using the Words & Phrases[48] search option. Begin with any

---

[44]   Right about now you're wondering to yourself if you are expected to cite to EVERYTHING. Even causal references to common sayings like, "sore thumb." Here's a link to the WikiPedia's answer to the origin of the saying, "sore thumb" https://en. wikipedia.org/wiki/Sore_Thumb.

[45]   If you try to find the origin for the phrase, "reasonable person" in BLACK'S, the only entry you'll find is (comically) within the definition of the absurdity doctrine, which reads: "[t]he principle that a provision in a legal instrument may be either disregarded or judicially corrected as an error (esp. when the correction is textually simple) if failing to do so would result in a disposition that no reasonable person could approve." Absurdity Doctrine, BLACK'S LAW DICTIONARY (11th ed. 2019).

[46]   BLACK'S LAW DICTIONARY (11th ed. 2019) is available in print and on Westlaw.

[47]   BALLENTINE'S LAW DICTIONARY (3rd ed. 2015) is available in print and on Lexis Advance®.

[48]   From the scope and coverage information note on WESTLAW, WORDS AND PHRASES, https://1.next.westlaw.com/Browse/Home/Cases/WordsandPhrases?origination Context=typeAhead&transitionType=CategoryPageItem&contextData=(sc.Default)#: "Words and Phrases contains judicial definitions, from both state and federal courts, from both published and unpublished opinions. Definitions may pertain to statutory language, court rules, administrative regulations, or business documents, among other sources. Each definition contains a citation from the court that provided the definition. Each definition is also classified by West's attorney-editors to the West Key

case law database—state or federal—and enter "wp" before your search phrase in parenthesis.

Westlaw Edge example, all state and federal cases:
wp("reasonable person")

Sort your results by Most Cited.[49]

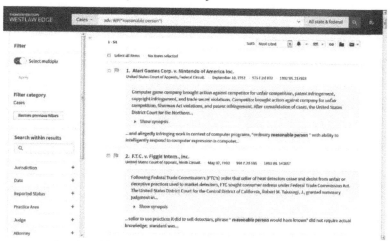

Reprinted from Westlaw with permission. Copyright 2019, Thomson Reuters. All rights reserved.

Interestingly, the Most Cited result in this example deals with a copyright issue, which is pretty close to the context of how I am using the reasonable person phrase. If you find there are a lot of cases (54!) that have defined your phrase, you may decide your phrase is so common, it does not need a citing reference.

Writing a scholarly article, or writing anything that involves legal analysis, is a process. If you are having trouble understanding a narrower issue, do more research. If you have trouble connecting

---

Number System(R), wherever possible*. New judicial constructions and interpretations of words and phrases are promptly supplied as they become available from the courts." Id.

[49] You can also search Words and Phrases on Westlaw by selecting Cases from the All Content Tab, then selecting Words & Phrases filter under the Tools & Resources options on the left.

your thoughts, do more research. Although research and writing are often taught as separate skills in separate courses, the two skills are dependent on one another. You cannot write a scholarly article without first adequately researching the issue. Hopefully the steps outlined above have helped you identify a unique issue you are excited to write about!

Table of Cases

Amendments to Rules
Regulating the Fla. Bar 4-1.1
& 6-10.3, In re, 167
American Small Business
League v. U.S. Small Bus.
Admin., 179
Biomet Inc. v. Finnegan
Henderson LLP, 166
Cass v. 1410088 Ontario Inc.,
179
Celotext Corp. v. Catrett, 143
Max Sound Corp. v. Google,
166
Maynard, People v., 166
Natural Gas Co. v. Apache
Corp., 168
Northwestern Nat. Ins. Co. v.
Guthrie, 166
Oracle Am., Inc. v. Google
Inc., 166
Oxfurth v. Siemens A.G., 166
Smith v. Lewis, 167
Vizio, Inc., Consumer Privacy
Litig., In re, 176
Woolley v. Hoffmann-La
Roche, Inc., 206
Zynga Game Networks v.
Ekran, 179